Pattern Fitting
with confidence

Nancy Zieman

Distributed in Canada by Fraser Direct
100 Armstrong Avenue
Georgetown, ON, Canada L7G 5S4
Tel: (905) 877-4411

Distributed in the U.K. and Europe by David & Charles
Brunel House, Newton Abbot, Devon, TQ12 4PU, England
Tel: (+44) 1626 323200, Fax: (+44) 1626 323319
E-mail: postmaster@davidandcharles.co.uk

Distributed in Australia by Capricorn Link
P.O. Box 704, S. Windsor, NSW 2756 Australia
Tel: (02) 4577-3555

Library of Congress Control Number: 2008925804
ISBN-13: 978-0-89689-574-4
ISBN-10: 0-89689-574-2

Edited by Jay Staten
Illustrations and Design: Laure Noe
Photographs: Dale Hall and Keith Glasgow
Nancy's Notions Editorial Staff: Pat Hahn and Diane Dhein

Manufactured in China.

13 12 11 10 09   5 4 3

PUBLISHER'S PREFACE

It is our great pleasure to publish Nancy Zieman's *Pattern Fitting with Confidence*. Like the previous books in the "with Confidence" series, this is an easy-to-understand, easy-to-implement guide, written by today's foremost expert. We know you will enjoy learning the techniques that will make your garment sewing successful every time.

Nancy Zieman celebrates the silver anniversary of her popular PBS television show *Sewing with Nancy*. It is a fitting time for this book to be published. Through 25 years, Nancy has guided her audience through the techniques that make us all better craftspeople. Her easygoing manner and "can do" attitude is part of every show, just has it has been part of every book she has written for Krause Publications.

We invite you to get started with *Pattern Fitting with Confidence*, making every garment a unique, well-tailored addition to your wardrobe.

Look for Nancy's other "with Confidence" books:

Quilt with Confidence
Machine Embroidery with Confidence
Serge with Confidence

And also

The Art of Landscape Quilting

by Nancy Zieman and Natalie Sewell

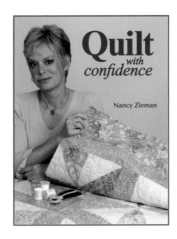
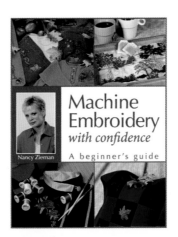

Table of Contents

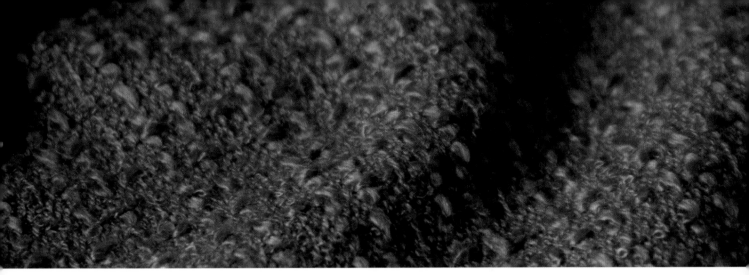

CHAPTER ONE

Getting Started

Fitting is definitely a sewing basic! If something doesn't fit, you won't wear it. Take a small amount of time and follow these step-by-step fitting techniques for a pattern that is "fit to be tried."

Choosing the Right Pattern Size

The first step to *pattern fitting with confidence* is to choose a pattern size that will give you the best fit. It is as simple as taking one measurement.

The common measurement used to choose pattern size for a blouse, jacket or top is your bust measurement. This measurement is accurate if your figure is well proportioned, but if your bust is large in proportion to the rest of your body or if you have a broad back, the bust measurement gives you a pattern that fits your bust but gaps at the neckline, the shoulders and the armholes. "Gaposis" is a common fitting problem that is difficult to correct. The solution? Buy your pattern to fit your shoulder area.

The measurement used in this book to determine which pattern size fits your shoulders is the *Right Size Measurement*, taken above the bustline between arm creases. You won't find the Right Size Measurement printed on the back of the pattern envelope, but it's quick to take and does not change even if you gain or lose weight.

NOTE FROM NANCY

I find the Right Size Measurement and other body measurements a challenge to take by myself, so I use the buddy system: I call a "sewing buddy" to help me, and I help her. This is the best way to ensure accuracy. Be sure to take the Right Size Measurement while you are wearing a camisole or leotard so that your arm creases are evident.

Choosing pattern size based on bust measurement can result in "gaposis."

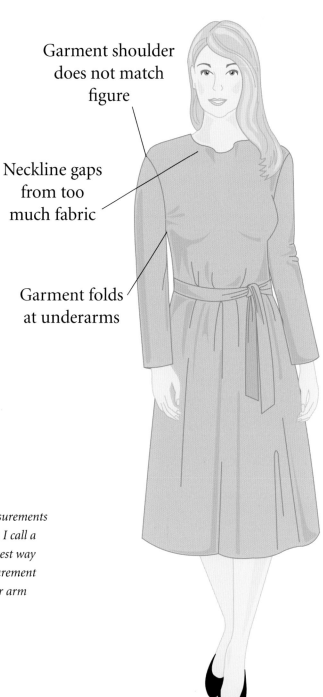

Garment shoulder does not match figure

Neckline gaps from too much fabric

Garment folds at underarms

Right Size Measurement

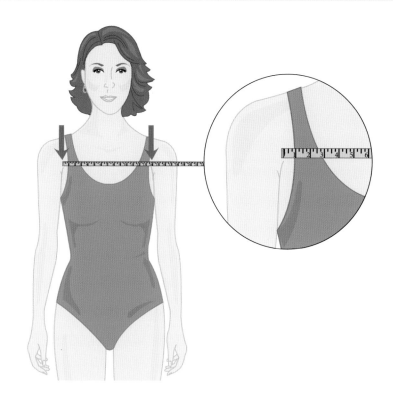

- Find the crease in your skin where your arm meets your body.

  - Measure above the end of one crease straight across the front chest to the end of the other crease.

  - Round off the measurement to the nearest ½".

Even though the Right Size Measurement and its corresponding sizes are not written on the back of the pattern envelope, the sizing is easy to remember. Misses' size 14 equals 14", and the sizes go up or down with every ½". For example, if your measurement is 13½", buy a size 12. If you measure 14½" select a size 16.

▌Note from Nancy

You may be pleasantly surprised by the results of the Right Size Measurement. It is common for someone who has been sewing with a size 20 pattern in order to fit her bust to find out she is actually a size 16!

If you are unsure which of two sizes to use, go with the smaller size. It is easier to increase the bustline on a pattern than to decrease the shoulder and neck area.

Right Size Measurement Fitting Chart

Measurement	12"	12½"	13"	13½"	14"	14½"	15"	15½"	16"	16½"	17"	17½"
Misses'/Petites	6	8	10	12	14	16	18	20	22			
Juniors	5	7	9	11	13	15						
Women's							38	40	42	44	46	48

Taking Accurate Measurements

You'll need to take five width measurements and two length measurements, in addition to the Right Size Measurement. (Pant measurements are slightly different; see pages 74–77 for details.) If you are buying a smaller size than you have in the past or if you are new to sewing, take all seven measurements. If your pattern size has not changed, consider measuring only the areas that you know are too tight, too loose, too long or too short.

Use the buddy system for taking all measurements.

■ NOTE FROM NANCY

Always measure to the closest ½" and don't get hung up on differences of ¼" or less! Our measurements fluctuate. (Just think what an extra piece of chocolate cake can do to the fit of your waistband.)

At the end of this book you'll find a *Personal Fitting Chart* on page 122. Using the guidelines below, record your measurements on the chart as you and your sewing buddy measure your figure. (Feel free to photocopy the fitting chart to use when fitting garments for friends and family.)

Bust

Measure around the fullest part of the bustline, keeping the tape measure parallel to the floor. Measure to the closest ½".

When taking width measurements, place a thumb or a finger underneath the tape measure to prevent the measurement from being taken too tightly.

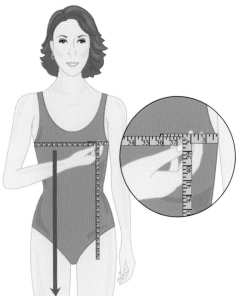

Waist

Bend to the side; the deepest resulting wrinkle is your waist. Stand straight again and measure around your waist, keeping the tape measure parallel to the floor. Place a thumb or a finger under the tape measure to prevent the measurement from being taken too tightly. Measure to the closest ½".

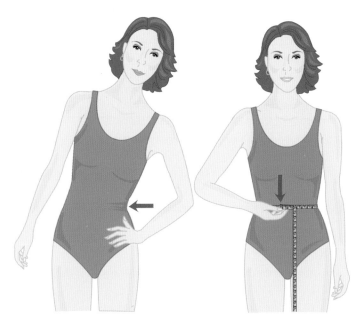

Hip

Measure the fullest part of the hip, keeping the tape measure parallel to the floor and a finger underneath the tape to make sure it is not too tight. Measure to the closest ½".

Hip Length

Take a second measurement—the hip length—measuring the distance between the waist and the hip. This measurement will let you mark hip placement, allowing you to add to or subtract from the pattern at your actual hip.

■ NOTE FROM NANCY

At the same time that I measure the width around my hip, I simply pick up the loose end of the tape measure to find the distance between my waist and hip.

Back Waist Length

Have your sewing buddy measure from the base of your neck to your waist. Find the base of your neck by bending your head forward until you easily feel the prominent bone at the base of the neck. Straighten your neck; your buddy can measure from that bone down your back to the waist.

Back Width

Have your sewing buddy measure from one side to the other across the back, directly above the back arm creases.

Sleeve Length

Feel for the knob at the end of your shoulder and keep a finger there. Depending on your body, it may help to raise your elbow as high as your shoulder. Place your hand on your hip. Have your sewing buddy measure from the shoulder knob over the elbow to your wrist bone. Measuring with your arm bent builds in ease for your sleeve.

Upper Arm Width

Have your sewing buddy measure the fullest part of your arm between the shoulder and the elbow, with a thumb or a finger underneath the tape measure to make sure it is not too tight. Measure to the closest ½".

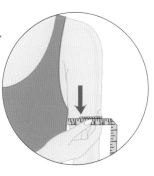

Choosing Your Pattern Type

Now that you know your correct size by using the Right Size Measurement, you have a choice of which type of pattern to buy—Misses', Miss Petite, Junior, Women's, or Women's Petite. For example, if your Right Size Measurement is 13½", you could buy a Misses' 12, or a Junior 11.

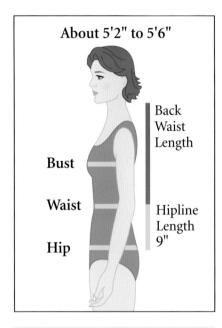

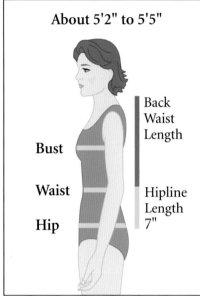

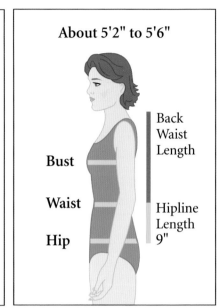

Misses'/Miss Petite:

These patterns are designed for well proportioned and well developed figures. Misses' are approximately 5'5" to 5'6" and Miss Petite are approximately 5'2" to 5'3", without shoes. Misses' back waist length is about 1" longer than a Miss Petite pattern.

Junior:

Junior patterns are designed for well proportioned, short waisted, figures who are about 5'2" to 5'5".

Women's/Women's Petite:

Women's and Women's Petite patterns have more room allotted in the bust, the waist, and the hip than Misses' patterns. Women's height is approximately 5'5" to 5'6", while the Women's Petite is approximately 5'2" to 5'3". The Women's back waist length is about 1" longer than a Women's Petite pattern.

NOTE FROM NANCY

Don't worry if your bust, waist, hip or back waist length are not the same as those in the charts. In this book, I'll show you how to adjust patterns easily.

Comparing Measurements

Now that you know your pattern size, type and body measurements, it's time to compare your measurements with those of your pattern. This information will guide you in making any pattern changes needed to attain a custom fit.

1 Create a Fitting Chart to record and analyze your measurements.

2 Check the back of the pattern envelope to determine pattern measurements for the size you selected. Record pattern bust, waist, hip and back waist length measurements. Then record your body measurements, as determined on pages 10–11.

	Pattern measurement	Body measurement	Change needed + or -
Bust			
Waist			
Hip			
Back waist length			
Upper arm			
Sleeve length			
Back width			

3 Compare pattern and body measurements for the bust, waist, hip and back waist length. Calculate the amount that must be added to or subtracted from each pattern measurement. For example, if the pattern envelope lists a 34" bust measurement, and your body measurement is 36", you need to add 2". If the pattern envelope lists a 26½" waist measurement, and your body measurement is 25½", you need to subtract 1".

	Pattern measurement	Body measurement	Change needed + or -
Bust	34"	36"	+2"
Waist	26-1/2"	25-1/2"	-1"
Hip	36"	39"	+3"
Back waist length	16-1/4"	16-1/4"	0
Upper arm			
Sleeve length			
Back width			

4 Upper arm (sleeve width) and sleeve length usually are not listed on the pattern envelope. Here's how to determine and compare those measurements:
- Upper arm (sleeve width):
  - To determine the pattern measurement, measure from pattern stitching line to pattern stitching line at the underarm seam.

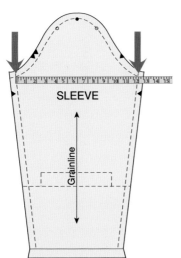

NOTE FROM NANCY
If you're using a multisized pattern, stitching lines may not be printed on the pattern. Check the pattern seam allowance. Measure and mark that distance from the cutting line at each underarm seam edge. Then measure from mark to mark. Round up to the nearest ½".

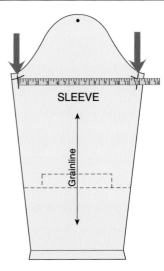

- Add ease to your body measurement. Garments need ease for comfort and movement. The measurement charts on the pattern envelope allow ease at the bust, waist and hips. A sleeve also needs ease. If you're using a woven fabric, add 2" to the body measurement for ease. For knit fabrics, add 1". Record that measurement on the chart.

	Pattern measurement	Body measurement	Change needed + or -
Bust	34"	36"	+2"
Waist	26-1/2"	25-1/2"	-1"
Hip	36"	39"	+3"
Back waist length	16-1/4"	16-1/4"	0
Upper arm	12"	12" + 1" = 13"	
Sleeve length			
Back width			

- Compare body upper arm measurement (body plus ease) to pattern sleeve width measurement. Calculate the difference to determine how much to add or subtract.

	Pattern measurement	Body measurement	Change needed + or -
Bust	34"	36"	+2"
Waist	26-1/2"	25-1/2"	-1"
Hip	36"	39"	+3"
Back waist length	16-1/4"	16-1/4"	0
Upper arm	12"	12" + 1" = 13"	+1"
Sleeve length			
Back width			

- Sleeve length: Measure the pattern from the large dot at the cap of the sleeve to the sleeve hemline. Compare that measurement to your body measurements; calculate the difference.

5 The back width measurement is not listed on the back of the envelope. If this is an area of fitting concern, you'll be making this fitting change after changing the pattern bust, if needed. You'll be measuring the changed pattern and then comparing measurements.

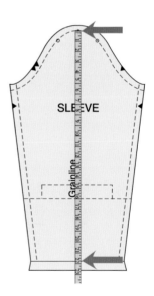

Choosing a Streamlined Style

For your first fitting project, choose a streamlined-style blouse, skirt, dress or jacket. By first trying the techniques on a basic pattern, you will learn methods of making your clothes fit that you can then easily use on other patterns.

A streamlined style means:

- Set-in sleeves
- Shoulder seams without a yoke
- No excessive gathering, tucking or pleating on the sleeves or the body
- Comfortably fitting jacket, not loose-fitting or oversize
- Straight, A-line or bias-cut skirt without excessive fullness

Once you know what adjustments to make on a streamlined-style pattern, you will automatically make those same changes on other patterns. Your *Personal Fitting Chart* is like a recipe to gain confidence on fitting patterns.

Allowing Design Ease

All patterns are designed with ease—a little extra room that gives both comfort and fashion. The amount of ease varies depending upon the style and the type of fabric for which the pattern was designed.

Design ease is the difference between the measurements on the back of the pattern, which apply to all patterns from that company, and the actual measurements of your tissue pattern, which apply only to the style you purchased.

The only time you need to check the pattern tissue measurements for the amount of design ease is when you think an oversized style may have extra inches of ease or a form-fitting style may not have enough ease for your comfort.

For woven fabrics, the minimum ease requirements to ensure a garment fits comfortably without binding are:

Bust:	3" to 4"
Waist	½" to 1"
Hip:	3" to 4"

Designers use these amounts as guidelines, varying the actual ease to give fashion and style to patterns. A loose-fitting jacket, for example, might have as much as 6" to 8" of bust ease.

Checking Design Ease

It's simple to check the design ease allowed in your pattern.

1 Pin the front and back pattern pieces together at the underarm, stacking the stitching lines.

2 Hold the tape measure with the 1" end in your left hand. Fold this end of the tape measure until it meets the bust measurement from the back of your pattern envelope. For example, if you are using a Misses' size 12, the bust measurement is 34".

3 Position the folded end of the tape measure across the bust area, measuring from the stitching (or fold) line of the center back to the stitching (or fold) line of the center front.

4 The gap between the 1" end of the tape measure and the stitching (or fold) line of the center front is half of the ease; double this measurement to find out the total design ease. Remember, you only need to check ease for tight or loose-fitting styles.

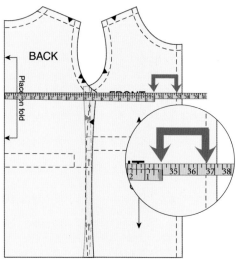

Design ease is extra room in the garment that gives both comfort and style

■ **NOTE FROM NANCY**
Some pattern companies print the actual pattern width on the tissue and the back of the pattern envelope, making the ease extremely simple to determine.

Learning to Pivot and Slide

You know what size you wear. You've recorded your body measurements, determined your figure silhouette, and selected a streamlined-style pattern. All you need now is to learn the pivot and slide techniques that will let you achieve *pattern fitting with confidence*.

◼ NOTE FROM NANCY

I've been sewing since the age of 10 and have tried practically every method of changing a pattern. I've slashed and spread, folded and tucked, and added a little at the seam allowances while cutting out the pattern. Needless to say, I've had a variety of successes and failures. Since I learned how to change a pattern with pivot and slide techniques, I haven't wavered. I know you'll have the same positive results.

Pattern designers use pivoting methods to make fashion changes. They move darts or add fullness by anchoring the basic pattern with a pin and moving the pattern in, out, and around. The pattern swings back and forth like the pendulum on a grandfather clock. Use this pivoting motion to change the pattern width.

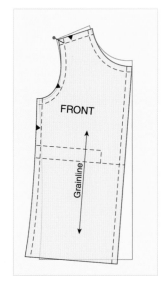

Pattern graders use the slide motion to change pattern sizes. They slide patterns up, down, and to the side to gradually increase or decrease from one size to the next. Use this sliding motion to add or subtract length.

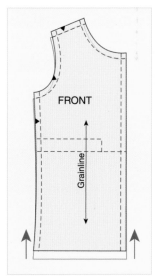

Pivot and slide techniques combine these two motions to fit a pattern simply, yet accurately. You make all of the changes on a worksheet (pattern paper or tissue paper), keeping the original pattern intact—no more cutting and taping! By changing the pattern equally on both sides of the grain, the seam and the design lines are kept in proportion to the original pattern. Best of all, each change is easy.

Organizing Your Fitting Tools

Fitting is streamlined with pivot and slide techniques. So are the tools you will need.

- Worksheets: Choose pattern tracing paper, waxed paper, or tissue paper. All pattern changes will be made on these sheets.

◼ NOTE FROM NANCY

When working with larger pattern pieces, tape two worksheets together or use 21" wide pattern paper. Pattern paper comes on a roll, and it's a real timesaver!

- Tools: Use two colors of pens (black and a second color) for tissue; a pencil and a tracing wheel for waxed paper. You will need two different marks on each worksheet—the original cutting line and the changes or adjustments. If you are using waxed paper as a worksheet, a tracing wheel and a pencil make it easy to transfer darts and grainlines. Work on a padded surface, such as an extra layer of fabric, and place the waxed paper and the pattern on top. The pencil and the tracing wheel will scratch off the wax and leave two distinctive marks.

- Basic tools: Use a tape measure, a ruler, tape and pins.

Getting Ready

Cut out the front, back, and sleeve (if applicable) pattern pieces along the cutting lines, eliminating notches. Press the pattern tissue pieces with a dry iron.

Cut a worksheet as long as each pattern piece. Don't worry if the waxed paper isn't wide enough. The worksheet only needs to extend to the side of the pattern as much as needed for the adjustment.

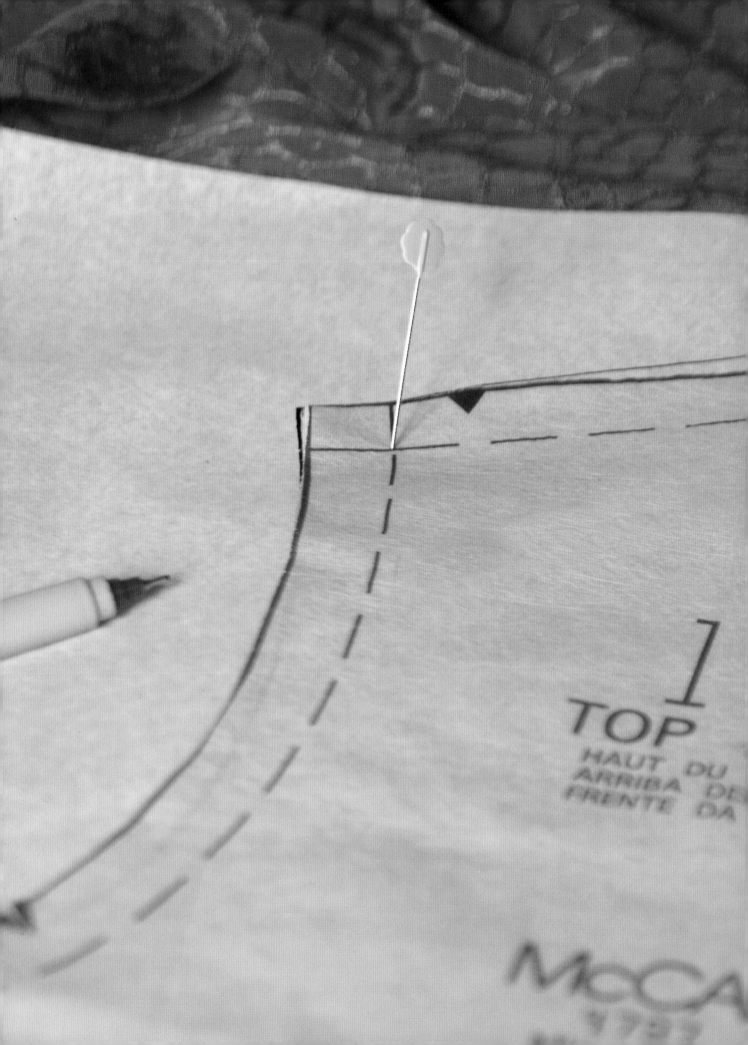

CHAPTER TWO

Basic Fitting Changes

The fitting solutions in this chapter will change your life—your pattern life! Once you've made basic changes to a pattern you will use it over and over again.

Bustline Changes

If your Personal Fitting Chart indicates a change of 1" or more, **divide that number by four** (the total number of cut edges at both side seams).

If you need to add more than a total of 4" to the bust width (1" per side seam), see page 57 for how to use extensions.

	Pattern measurement	Body measurement	Change needed + or -
Bust	34"	36"	+2"
Waist	26-1/2"	25-1/2"	-1"
Hip	36"	39"	+3"
Back waist length	16-1/4"	16-1/4"	0
Upper arm	12"	12" + 1" = 13"	+1"
Sleeve length	22"	21"	-1"
Back width	18"	19"	+1"

■ NOTE FROM NANCY

I quickly determine the fitting change at each cut edge by creating a simple fraction, placing the change over the number of cut edges. For example, if you need to add 3" and the number of cut edges is 4, the amount to add per edge would be ¾". Presto!

Increasing Bustline

1 Place the front pattern piece on a worksheet; outline the cutting lines of the pattern on the worksheet using a black marker. Measure the needed increase out at the underarm cutting line; mark.

2 Place a pin at the stitching line where the shoulder and armhole intersect. Pivot the pattern out to the increase mark. Trace the new armhole cutting line with a colored marker, mark the notches.

3 Keeping the pattern pivoted, move the pin to the stitching line where the armhole and side seam intersect. Pivot the pattern in to the original outlined waist. Trace the new cutting line between the underarm and the waist; mark the notches.

4 Match the pattern to the original outline and tape it to the worksheet. Cut out the pattern, following the new outline.

5 Repeat steps 1 through 4 on the back pattern piece.

■ NOTE FROM NANCY

When you place the pattern in its original position, notice the change. The bust width is increased, but the armhole is the same size as the original pattern. Plus, your pattern is still intact.

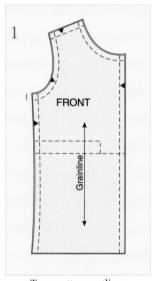

Trace pattern outline; mark increase.

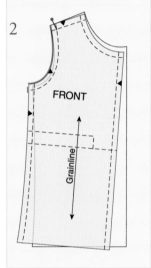

Pivot to increase mark; trace armhole.

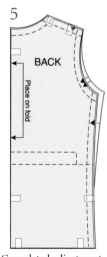

Pivot to waist; trace side.

Completed adjustment

Decreasing Bustline

1 Place the front pattern piece on a worksheet; outline the cutting lines of the pattern. Measure the needed decrease in from the underarm cutting line; mark.

2 Place a pin at the stitching line where the shoulder and armhole intersect. Pivot the pattern in to the decrease mark. Trace the new armhole cutting line; mark the notches.

3 Keeping the pattern pivoted, move the pin to the stitching line where the armhole and side seam intersect. Pivot the pattern out to the original waist. Trace the new cutting line between the underarm and the waist; mark the notches.

4 Match the pattern to the original outline. Fold in the pattern sections that overlap the new outline; tape. Cut out the pattern, following the new outline.

5 Repeat steps 1 through 4 on the back pattern piece.

	Pattern measurement	Body measurement	Change needed + or -
Bust	34"	33"	-1"
Waist	26-1/2"	27-1/2"	+1"
Hip	36"	37"	+2"
Back waist length	16-1/4"	16-1/4"	0
Upper arm	12"	12" + 1" = 13"	+1"
Sleeve length	22"	21"	-1"
Back width	18"	19"	+1"

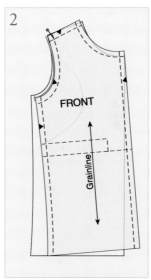

Trace pattern outline; mark decrease.

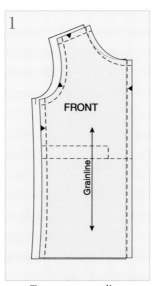

Pivot to decrease mark; trace armhole.

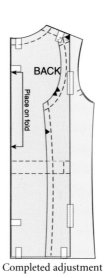

Pivot to waist; trace side.

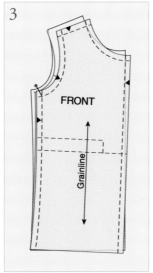

Completed adjustment

Bustline Changes, continued

Fitting the Bustline with
Three Main Pattern Pieces

Just when you think you've mastered fitting the bust, you come across a jacket pattern with not two, but *three* main body pieces: the front, the back and the side panel. Don't worry; basic pivoting techniques still apply.

Change only the front and back pieces; the width of the side panel pattern piece remains the same. Yet, you'll need to mark a reference line. Here are the changes:

1 Mark an underarm reference line. Pin the front, side panel and back pattern pieces together at the underarm stitching lines. Extend a line perpendicular to the grainline as illustrated.

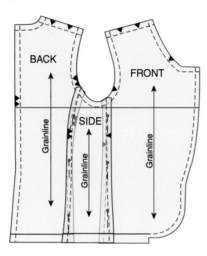

2 Outline the patterns and mark the needed increase on separate worksheets. Measure the needed increase out from the underarm cutting line on both the front and back pieces; mark. (If decreasing, measure in from the cutting line.)

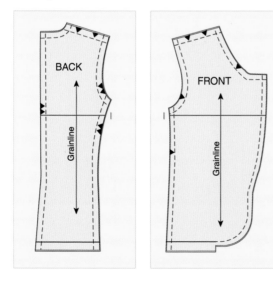

3 Pivot twice to increase the new armhole and side seam, as detailed on the previous page, but use the underarm line as the second pivot point.

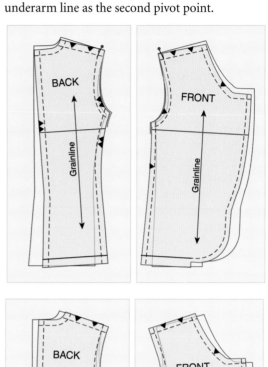

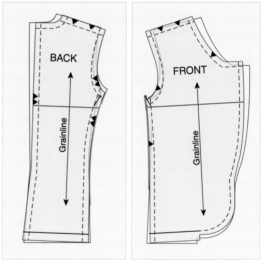

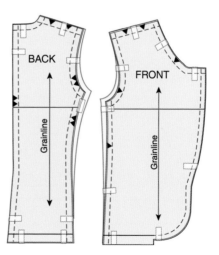

Dart Changes

Lowering the Bust Dart

This simple modification moves the entire dart down without changing the length of the pattern. Determine the change by marking your bust position on the pattern.

Determining Changes

1 Pin the front and back pattern pieces together at the shoulder seam, stacking stitching lines. Pin the pattern to the shoulder area and center front of your camisole or leotard. On the pattern, gently mark the fullest part of your bust with an X. Unpin and remove the pattern.

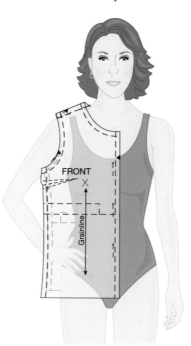

2 On the front pattern piece, use a ruler to extend the upper dart leg (Y) toward the center front. Measure the distance between this extended line and your bust point X marked on the pattern. Write this bust dart change measurement on the pattern and make a note on your Personal Fitting Chart, page 122. Outline the cutting lines of the neck, shoulder, and armhole on a worksheet. Do not outline the side seam.

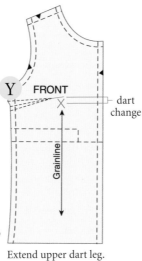

Extend upper dart leg.

3 Slide the pattern down at the side seam the amount noted in step 2. Trace the new side seam. Make hash marks (points Y and Z) at the side seam to mark the beginning of each dart leg.

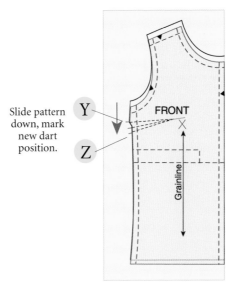

Slide pattern down, mark new dart position.

4 Place a worksheet on top of the pattern, aligning the colored lines with the pattern's side seams. Using the pattern piece as a guide, trace the dart legs on the worksheet. The dart is the same size; it has simply been moved down.

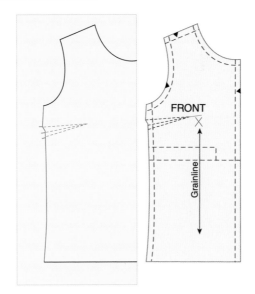

5 Tape the worksheet on top of the pattern so that the changed dart is evident. Cut out the pattern, following the new outline.

■ NOTE FROM NANCY
Reverse the process if raising a dart.

Dart Changes, continued

Adding a Dart

If you have noticed that in tops or a blouse without darts, the waist pulls up, and bias wrinkles radiate from the underarm to the bust, consider adding a dart.

1 Pin the front and back pattern pieces together at the shoulder seam, stacking stitching lines. Tape a worksheet on top of the front pattern piece below the underarm; extend the worksheet at the side and the bottom. Pin the pattern to the shoulder area and to the center front of your camisole or leotard. On the pattern, gently mark the fullest part of your bust with an X.

2 At the side seam, fold the pattern and worksheet to form the bust dart. The fold should be deep enough to allow the center front of your pattern to hang straight. Pin the dart closed. Remove the pattern, leaving the dart pinned and the worksheet taped to the pattern. Measure and record the full depth of the dart at the side seam. The full depth is twice the folded measurement.

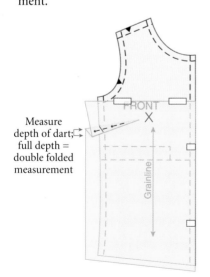

Measure depth of dart; full depth = double folded measurement

3 Unpin the dart; draw line X on the worksheet from bust point X to the side seam, making a line perpendicular to the grainline. Line X is merely a starting point and does not become part of the dart.

- On the worksheet, measure 1" down from line X at the underarm.
- Measure 1" from bust point X along line X; mark, extending the line downward ½".
- Draw the first dart leg Y at an angle toward the fullest part of the bust, beginning at the underarm and stopping 1" before the bust point.
- Measure down from the first dart leg Y the full depth of the dart measured in step 2; mark point Z. Draw a line at an angle from point Z to the end of line Y, forming the dart.

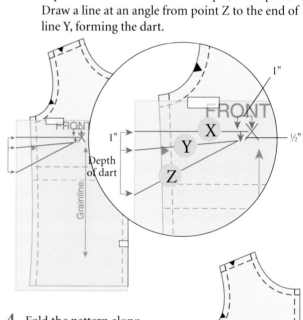

4 Fold the pattern along dart leg Z to meet dart leg Y to determine the dart underlay. Keeping the dart folded, draw a straight line along the side seam cutting line between the pattern underarm and waist.

Cut the pattern and the worksheet along this line and unfold. Voilà! The dart underlay and the length of the dart leg were both made at the same time.

5 On the worksheet, add the depth of the dart to the hem allowance across the bottom of the front piece. Cut out the rest of the pattern, following the new outline.

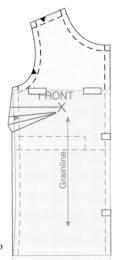

Add depth of dart to hem allowance.

Increasing the Dart Size

Misses' patterns are designed to fit a B cup; Juniors, an A/B cup; Women's Petite, a C cup; and Women's, a D cup. Dart depth increases ½" per cup size. You may have the proportions to wear a Misses' pattern, but need a deeper dart. This method deepens the dart and automatically adds needed length to the center front. You'll be pleased to see how easy it is to make this change and how well the pattern fits.

1 Outline the front pattern piece lower edge and center front (or center cut edge).

2 Slide the pattern up ½" for each needed cup size increase. For example, to change a Misses' B-cup size to a D-cup size, slide the pattern up 1"; to change to a C-cup size, slide the pattern up ½". Outline the neck, shoulder, armhole, and side seams to the first dart leg Y. Place a hash mark at dart leg Y.

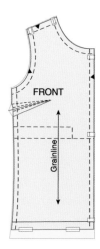

Slide pattern up; mark upper dart leg.

3 Slide the pattern down to the original lower outline of the pattern bottom. Place a hash mark at lower dart leg Z and continue to trace the side seam.

4 Draw the new dart legs.

- Match the pattern to the outline marks at the shoulder area on the worksheet; tape. Use hash mark Z made in step 3 to draw a new lower dart leg to the original dart point.

- Treating the worksheet and the pattern as one, fold the lower dart leg to meet the top leg. Draw the new cutting line between the underarm and the second dart leg.

- Cut out the worksheet, following the new side seam cutting line. The dart underlay will be slightly wider due to the deeper dart.

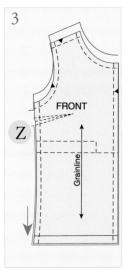

Slide pattern down; mark lower dart leg.

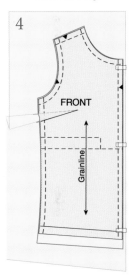

5 Unfold the dart. Cut out the pattern, following the new outline.

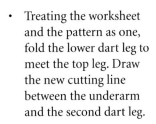

Hipline Changes

If your Personal Fitting chart indicates a change of 1" or more, **divide the needed change by four** (the total number of cut edges). For example, if you need to increase the hipline 3" and there are four seam edges, add ¾" to each edge.

	Pattern measurement	Body measurement	Change needed + or -
Bust	34"	36"	+2"
Waist	26-1/2"	25-1/2"	-1"
Hip	36"	39"	+3"
Back waist length	16-1/4"	16-1/4"	0
Upper arm	12"	12" + 1" = 13"	+1"
Sleeve length	22"	21"	-1"
Back width	18"	19"	+1"

Fitting a One-Piece Dress

1. Outline the front pattern piece on a worksheet. Using your hip length measurement, draw a hipline perpendicular to the grainline. Measure the needed increase out from the hipline; mark. Measure the same increase out from the side seam cutting line at the lower edge of the dress; mark. For a decrease, measure in at both the hip and the hem.

2. Place a pin at the stitching line where the waist and side seam intersect. Pivot the pattern to the mark at the hip. Trace the new cutting line between the waist and the hip.

3. Keeping the pattern pivoted, move the pin to the stitching line at the hipline mark; pivot the pattern to the mark at the hem. Trace between the hip and hem.

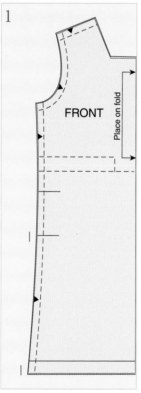

Outline pattern; mark increase at hip and at hem.

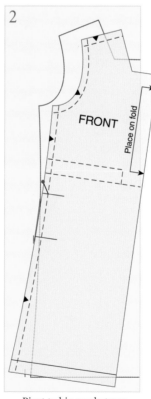

Pivot to hip mark; trace between waist and hip.

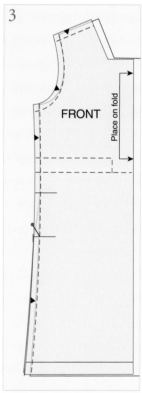

Pivot to hem mark; trace between hip and hem.

4 Match the pattern to the original outline; tape. If decreasing, fold in the pattern sections that overlap the new outline. Cut out the pattern, following the new outline.

5 Repeat steps 1 through 4 on the back pattern piece.

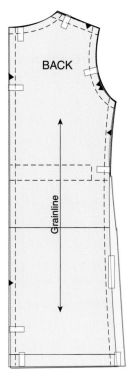

NOTE FROM NANCY

If you're sewing a jacket with a side panel and need to increase the hipline, alter only the front and back pattern pieces, not the side panel. This involves four cut edges, so you can use the same hip changes as detailed on page 26.

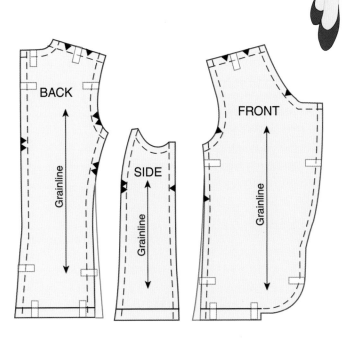

Waistline Changes

If your Personal Fitting Chart indicates a change of 1" or more, **divide the needed change by four**, the number of cut edges at both side seams. For example, if you need to increase the waistline 2", you would add ½" to each cut edge.

	Pattern measurement	Body measurement	Change needed + or -
Bust	34"	35"	+1"
Waist	26-1/2"	28-1/2"	+2"
Hip	36"	38"	+2"
Back waist length	16-1/4"	16-1/4"	0
Upper arm	12"	12" + 1" = 13"	+1"
Sleeve length	22"	21"	-1"
Back width	18"	19"	+1"

Increasing a Fitted Waist

1 Outline the front pattern piece on a worksheet.

2 Measure out from the waist for the increase; mark.

3 Place a pin at the stitching line where the armhole and side seam intersect. Pivot the pattern out to the increase mark. Trace the new cutting line.

4 Match the pattern to the original outline; tape. Cut out the pattern, following the new outline.

5 Repeat steps 1 through 4 on the back pattern piece.

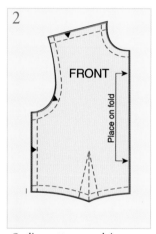 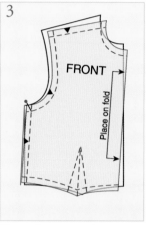 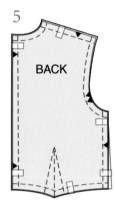

Outline pattern; mark increase.   Pivot to increase mark; trace new cutting line.

Decreasing a Fitted Waist

1 Outline the front pattern piece on a worksheet.

2 Measure in at the waist for the decrease amount; mark.

3 Place a pin at the stitching line where the armhole and side seam intersect. Pivot the pattern in to the decrease mark. Trace the new cutting line.

4 Match the pattern to the original outline; tape. Fold in the pattern sections that overlap the new outline. Cut out the pattern, following the new outline.

5 Repeat steps 1 through 4 on the back pattern piece.

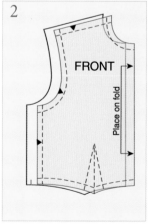 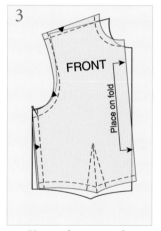

Outline pattern; mark decrease.   Pivot to decrease mark; trace new cutting line.

NOTE FROM NANCY
Avoid over-fitting your patterns. It isn't necessary to be exact to within ⅛" nor to remove every wrinkle. Over-fitting can be exasperating and can take the joy out of sewing.

Sleeve Changes

If your Personal Fitting Chart indicates a change of more than ½", divide the increase by two (the total number of cut edges). For example, if you need 1½", add ¾" at each cut edge of the sleeve.

To increase more than 2" (1" per cut edge), add extensions (see page 57).

	Pattern measurement	Body measurement	Change needed + or -
Bust	34"	35"	+1"
Waist	26-1/2"	28-1/2"	+2"
Hip	36"	38"	+2"
Back waist length	16-1/4"	16-1/4"	0
Upper arm	12"	13-1/2"	+1-1/2"
Sleeve length	22"	21"	-1"
Back width	18"	19"	+1-1/2"

Increasing Short Sleeves

1   Outline the sleeve pattern piece on a worksheet. Measure the needed increase out from the cutting lines on both sides of the pattern (in the example, ¾"); mark.

2   Place a pin at the stitching line at the top of the sleeve; pivot the pattern to either increase mark. Trace half of the sleeve cap and 1" along the side seam. Do not draw the entire cutting line.

3   Pivot the pattern to the second increase mark; trace the other half of the sleeve cap and 1" along the side cutting line.

4   Remove the pin; slide the pattern horizontally along the hemline to the portion of the side cutting line traced in step 2. Trace the new side cutting line. Repeat on the other side.

5   Match the pattern to the original outline; tape. Cut out the pattern, following the new outline.

Decreasing Short Sleeves

To decrease the width of a short sleeve, pivot the pattern in to the decrease mark; trace on the worksheet. Repeat for the opposite side. Slide the pattern horizontally to the decrease marks and finish outlining the new side cutting lines.

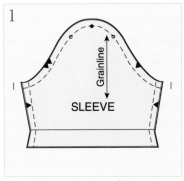

Outline pattern; mark increase on both sides.

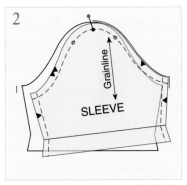

Pivot to increase mark; trace half of sleeve cap and 1" along side seam.

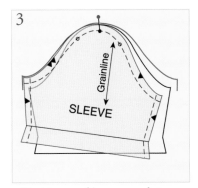

Pivot to second increase mark; trace other half of sleeve cap and 1" along side seam.

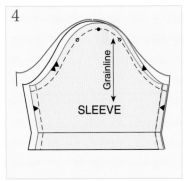

Slide pattern horizontally; trace new side cutting line.

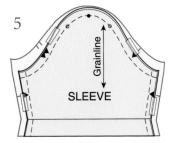

Cut out pattern following new outline.

Sleeve Changes, *continued*

Increasing Long Sleeves

1 Outline the sleeve pattern piece on a worksheet. Measure the needed increase out from both side seams (in the example on page 29, ¾"). Mark increases at the underarms parallel to both side seams.

2 Place a pin at the stitching line at the top of the sleeve; pivot the pattern to one increase mark. Trace half of the sleeve cap and 1" of the side cutting line. Do not draw the entire side cutting line.

3 Keeping the pattern pivoted, move the pin to the stitching line where the sleeve cap and side seam intersect. Pivot the pattern so that the bottom of the sleeve meets the original cutting line. Trace the new side cutting line, which gradually tapers to the original line at the hem.

4 Repeat steps 2 and 3 for the second side of the long sleeve.

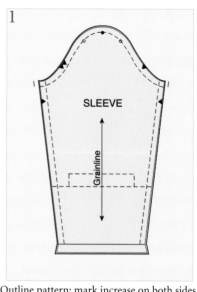

Outline pattern; mark increase on both sides.

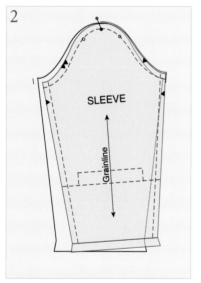

Pivot to increase mark; trace sleeve cap.

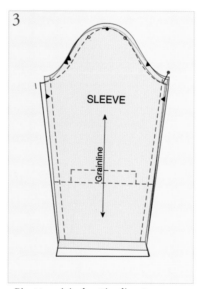

Pivot to original cutting line; trace new cutting line.

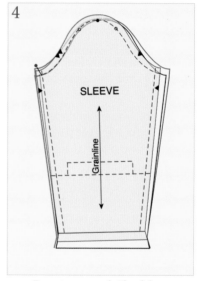

Repeat on second side of sleeve.

5 Match the pattern to the original outline; tape. Cut out the pattern, following the new outline.

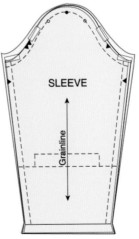

NOTE FROM NANCY

You can decrease the width of a long sleeve by following the same steps as above, but the decrease marks will be inside the pattern cutting lines, and your worksheet will end up smaller than the pattern.

Increasing Two-Piece Sleeves

When increasing the width on a two-piece sleeve, all of the extra width is added to the upper sleeve. The sleeve still fits perfectly into the armhole of your jacket.

If your Personal Fitting Chart indicates a change of more than ½", divide the increase by two (the total number of cut edges). For example, if you need 1½", add ¾" at each cut edge of the sleeve.

To increase more than 2" (1" per cut edge), add extensions (see page 57).

1 Draw a reference line, outline the pattern, and mark the increase.
   - Pin sleeve pattern pieces together at the underarm seam, stacking stitching lines. Draw a line perpendicular to the grainline from the underarm seam of the under sleeve to the upper sleeve side seam.

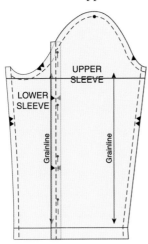

   - Unpin the pattern pieces.
   - Outline the upper sleeve pattern piece on a worksheet. Measure the needed increase out on both sides at the underarm line; mark.

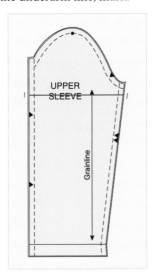

2 Modify the sleeve pattern as detailed on the previous page.

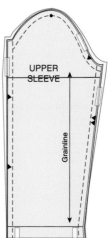

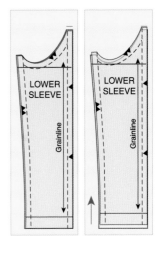

NOTE FROM NANCY

If a large amount is added to the pattern at each side (1" or more) the length of the underarm seam may grow. Measure the distance between the original outline and the cutting line on the upper sleeve at the underarm seam, then adjust the under sleeve by that measurement. See lengthening changes, pages 44–45.

Adjust under sleeve by this measurement.

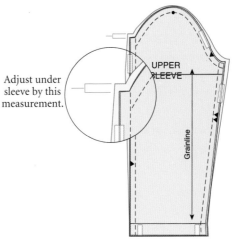

Shoulder Changes

The key to a great fit is starting with the correct pattern size. The *Right Size Measurement Fitting Chart*, page 9, gives you a proportioned fit in the shoulder, the armhole, and the neck. That means droopy shoulders, gaping necklines, and large armholes should be fitting challenges of the past. Yet, you may need to fine-tune the fit in the shoulders if you have narrow, broad, sloping or square shoulders.

It is impossible to measure a shoulder and determine a change. Why? Shoulder seams are style features—jackets, blouses, vests and tops all have varying degrees of shoulder lengths. Use a common sense approach to fitting narrow, broad, sloping or square shoulders.

The comfort of your clothes is the best indicator of a good or poor shoulder fit.

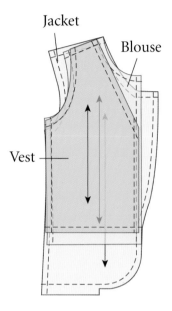

Narrow Shoulders
Sleeves hang off the shoulders.

Broad Shoulders
Stress wrinkles appear at the sleeve areas on both the front and back.

For all four shoulder changes, the Common Sense approach to fitting is to change the length or angle of the shoulder ¼" or ½".

NOTE FROM NANCY

A ¼" or ½" may not seem like a major change. Consider that the average shoulder width is only 5". A ½" adjustment results in a 10 percent change—which will be very useful!

Square Shoulders
Garment rides up at the neck, creating stress wrinkles.

Sloping Shoulders
Sleeves bind or folds form at the underarm.

Narrow Shoulders

If the sleeves hang off the shoulders, you may have narrow shoulders. Yet, if your *Right Size Pattern* is a smaller size than you've used in the past, the shoulders will automatically be narrower! If you still believe you need a narrow shoulder change, **make only ¼" or ½" change.** This is a common sense approach. . . you be the judge.

1   Outline the front pattern piece on a worksheet. Measure the needed decrease amount in from the shoulder cutting line; mark.

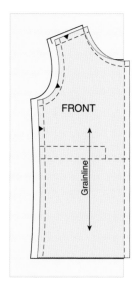

Narrow shoulders cause
sleeves to hang off shoulders.

4   Align the pattern with the original outline. Tape, leaving the armhole area free. Fold in sections that overlap the new outline. Cut out the pattern, following the new outline.

NOTE FROM NANCY

The modified armhole is the same size as the original armhole. It may appear slightly higher, but it will fit correctly.

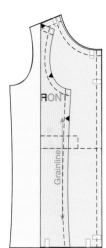

2   Align the pattern with the outline; slide the pattern along the shoulder seam so that the shoulder cutting line meets the decrease mark.

3   Insert a pin at the stitching line where the shoulder and armhole intersect. Pivot the pattern out to the original underarm cutting line. Trace the new armhole.

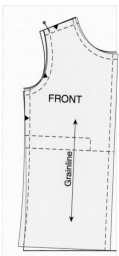

5   Repeat steps 1 through 4 on the back pattern piece.

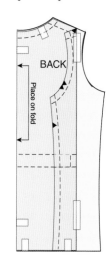

Broad Shoulders

If you have stress wrinkles at the sleeve on both the front and the back of your garments, you have broad shoulders. **Change the angle of the shoulder by ¼" or ½".**

Broad shoulders cause
stress wrinkles.

1 Outline the front pattern piece on a worksheet. Measure the needed increase out from the shoulder; mark.

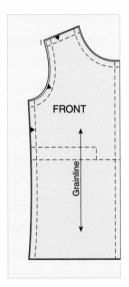

2 Slide the pattern along the shoulder seam so that the shoulder cutting line meets the increase mark. Trace the wider shoulder cutting line.

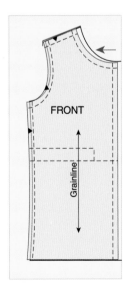

3 Place a pin at the stitching line where the shoulder and armhole intersect. Pivot the pattern in to the original underarm cutting line. Trace the new armhole cutting line.

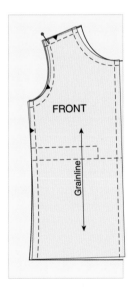

4 Match the pattern to the original outline. Cut out the pattern, following the new outline.

5 Repeat steps 1 through 4 on the back pattern piece.

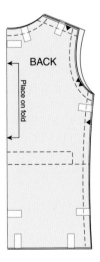

Square Shoulders

Your best cue as to whether you should make pattern changes for square shoulders is the fit of an existing garment. If your garment rides up at the neck, creating stress wrinkles at the shoulders and causing the neckline to feel too loose, you have square shoulders. **Change the angle of the shoulder by ¼" or ½".**

Square shoulders cause stress wrinkles at neck.

Determining Changes

1 Outline the front pattern piece cutting lines on a worksheet. Measure ¼" or ½" up from the end of the shoulder; mark.

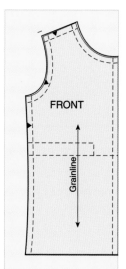

3 Keeping the pattern pivoted, move the pin to the stitching line where the shoulder and armhole intersect. Pivot the pattern in to the original underarm outline. Trace the new armhole cutting line.

4 Match the pattern to the original outline; tape. Cut out the pattern, following the new outline.

5 Repeat steps 1 through 4 on the back pattern piece.

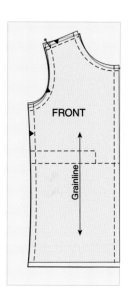

2 Insert a pin at the stitching lines where the neck and shoulder intersect. Pivot the pattern out to the increase mark. Trace the new shoulder cutting line.

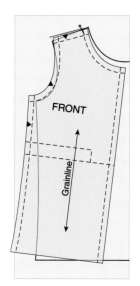

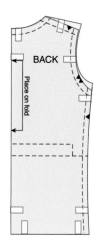

Sloping Shoulders

Sloping shoulders cause clothing to bind or folds to form at the underarm. **Change the angle of the shoulder ¼" or ½".**

Sloping shoulders cause folds at underarms.

1 Outline the front pattern piece on a worksheet. Measure down ¼" or ½" from the end of the shoulder cutting line; mark.

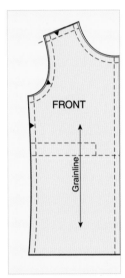

2 Place a pin at the stitching line where the neck and shoulder intersect. Pivot the pattern down to the decrease mark. Trace the new shoulder cutting line.

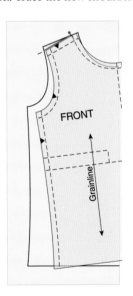

3 Keeping the pattern pivoted, move the pin to the stitching line where the shoulder and armhole intersect. Pivot in to the original underarm outline. Trace the new armhole.

4 Match the pattern to the original outline and fold in the sections that overlap the new outline; tape. Cut out the pattern, following the new outline.

5 Repeat steps 1 through 4 on the back pattern piece.

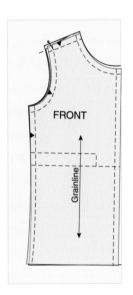

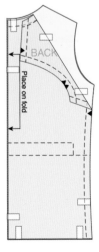

NOTE FROM NANCY

The new pattern armhole slopes at a greater angle to match your body shape. This prevents the garment from binding at the underarms and eliminates folds caused by sloping shoulders.

One Shoulder Lower Than the Other

It is fairly common to have one shoulder lower than the other. In this case, make the fitting changes after cutting out the pattern.

1. Cut the front and back pattern pieces from your fabric without making any shoulder adjustments. Unpin the pattern pieces from the fabric.

2. Make sloping shoulder changes on worksheets, following the steps shown on page 36.

3. On the right (not wrong) side of your fabric, match the worksheet pattern to the fabric **only on the side that corresponds to the sloping shoulder**. Double check before you cut to be sure you cut the correct shoulder. Recut both the front and the back of your garment, using the worksheet as a cutting guide.

Bias wrinkles on only one side indicate that only one shoulder slopes.

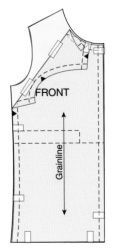

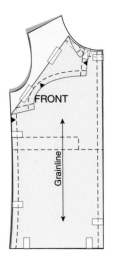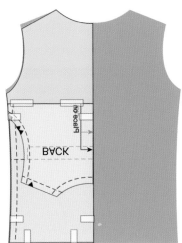

Back Changes

Adding Fullness

A common fitting complaint is tightness across the back. Many of us buy a larger pattern size just to improve the fit across the back only to discover that we then have a poor fit through the neck and the shoulders. Here is a way to add room across the back without purchasing a larger size.

Determining Changes

If you have already added an increase at the bust, you may not need to change your pattern to add back fullness. When pivoting, half of any amount added to the bust is automatically added to the back width. For example, if you add 1" at each side seam to increase the bust, the back width increases ½" per side seam or a total of 1".

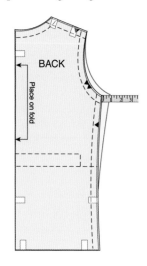

Tightness across the back causes horizontal pull wrinkles.

If you did not increase the bust, or if you need even more back width, measure your pattern to determine the amount to add.

- Add 1½" of "ease" to your back width measurement recorded on your Personal Fitting Chart, page 122.

- Mark this measurement on your tape measure with your thumbnail. Fold the end of your tape measure to this mark.

- Measure from the center back of your pattern across to the dot at the center of the armhole stitching line. If you increased the bust, measure your modified pattern.

- The distance between the 1" end of the tape measure and the armhole stitching line is the amount you need to add across the back pattern piece.

- Add the same increase at the center of the armhole and at the underarm to give the needed width for a broad back.

	Pattern measurement	Body measurement	Change needed + or -
Bust	34"	36"	+2"
Waist	26-1/2"	25-1/2"	-1"
Hip	36"	39"	+3"
Back waist length	16-1/4"	16-1/4"	0
Upper arm	12"	12" + 1" = 13"	+1"
Sleeve length	22"	21"	-1"
Back width	18"	19"	1 + 1-1/2" ease

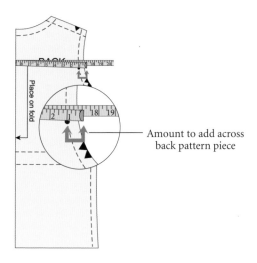

Amount to add across back pattern piece

1 Outline the back pattern piece on a worksheet. Measure out the needed increase from both the center of the armhole **and** the underarm cutting line, mark.

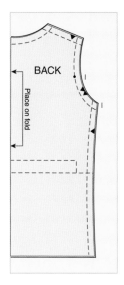

■ **NOTE FROM NANCY**
This is one of the few times you add in two areas for one fitting change.

2 Place a pin at the stitching line where the shoulder and armhole intersect. Pivot the pattern out to the first increase mark at the center mark on your worksheet. Trace the new armhole to the center mark on the worksheet.

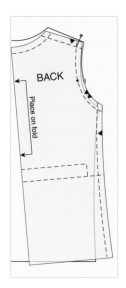

3 Keeping the pattern pivoted, move the pin to the stitching line at the center of the armhole. Pivot the pattern out to the increase mark at the underarm. Trace the remaining armhole section.

4 Keeping the pattern pivoted, move the pin to the stitching line where the armhole and side seam intersect. Pivot the pattern in to the original waistline. Trace the new cutting line at the side seam.

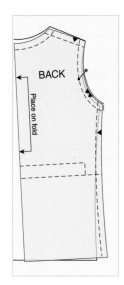

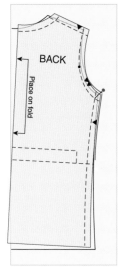

5 Match the pattern to the original outline; tape. Cut out the pattern, following the new outline.

■ **NOTE FROM NANCY**
The new armhole cutting line is not as "C-shaped" as the original pattern, but it is the same length. You do not have to make any adjustments to the front pattern piece because the back side seam did not change in length.

Back Changes, *continued*

Curved Back

For people with a curved back or rounded shoulders, the waist length of the back pattern piece needs to be lengthened. If your Personal Fitting Chart indicates a change of ½" or more, change the pattern back.

	Pattern measurement	Body measurement	Change needed + or -
Bust	34"	36"	+2"
Waist	26-1/2"	25-1/2"	-1"
Hip	36"	39"	+3"
Back waist length	16	16-1/2"	+1/2"
Upper arm	12"	12" + 1" = 13"	+1"
Sleeve length	22"	21"	-1"
Back width	18"	19"	+/-1/2"

Vertical wrinkles occur when back waist length is too short.

1. Outline the back pattern piece on a worksheet. Measure the needed length up from the neck cutting line at the center back; mark.

2. Slide the pattern up to the increase mark. Trace the longer center back and neck cutting lines.

3. Keeping the pattern in a raised position, place a pin at the stitching line where the neck and shoulder intersect. Pivot the pattern to the original outline at the end of the shoulder. Trace the new shoulder cutting line.

4. Match the pattern to the original outline; tape. Cut out the pattern, following the new outline.

5. If the pattern has a shoulder dart, extend the dart legs to meet the new shoulder cutting line. Longer shoulder darts are needed for rounded shoulders. If the pattern doesn't have a shoulder dart, the back shoulder seam might be slightly longer. When stitching the shoulder seams, ease the back shoulder seam to fit the front shoulder seam.

Outline; mark change.

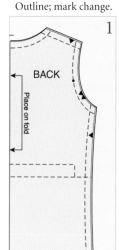

Slide pattern up; trace.

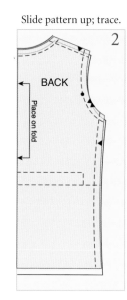

Pivot to shoulder end; trace.

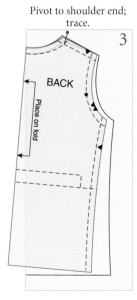

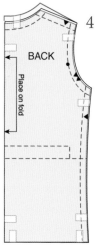

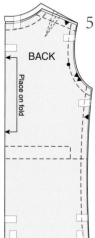

Swayback

The back pattern piece needs to be shorter for people with a swayback or very erect posture. Wrinkles that gather at the back waist indicate that the back waist length is too long.

If your Personal Fitting Chart indicates a change of ½" or more, change the pattern back.

	Pattern measurement	Body measurement	Change needed + or -
Bust	34"	36"	+2"
Waist	26-1/2"	25-1/2"	-1"
Hip	36"	39"	+3"
Back waist length	16-1/2"	16	-1/2"
Upper arm	12"	12" + 1" = 13"	+1"
Sleeve length	22"	21"	-1"
Back width	18"	19"	+1-1/2"

Horizontal wrinkles occur when back waist length is too long.

1 Outline the back pattern piece on a worksheet. Measure the needed decrease down from the cutting line at the center back; mark.

2 Slide the pattern down to the decrease mark. Trace the new neckline.

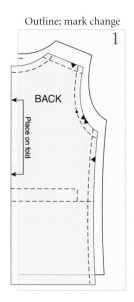

Outline; mark change

Slide pattern down; trace

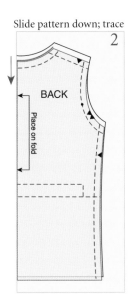

3 Keeping the pattern in a lowered position, place a pin at the stitching line where the neck and shoulder intersect. Pivot the pattern to the original outline at the end of the shoulder seam. Trace the new shoulder cutting line.

4 Match the pattern to the original outline; tape. Fold in the pattern sections that overlap the new outline.

5 Cut out the pattern, following the new outline.

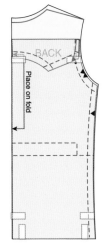

■ NOTE FROM NANCY
Only the back pattern piece needs to be pivoted at the neck to correct for a curved back or for a swayback. With this method the back side seams remain the same length as the front side seams and the neckline does not change, so the collar fits the adjusted pattern.

Hemline Changes

Use sliding techniques to change the pattern length. To keep your pattern proportional, extend the grainline or a line perpendicular to the grain and use it as a guide when sliding your pattern up, down, right, or left.

Determining Changes

Pin the front and back pattern pieces together at the shoulder seams, stacking stitching lines.

Pin the front pattern piece's shoulder seam and center front to your camisole or leotard. Mark your waistline at the front and the back with your sewing buddy's help.

Walk the pattern down your figure, pinch the pattern at the desired length, and mark it with a pencil. Unpin the pattern.

Using the hem allowance printed near the pattern's hem cutting line, draw a new hemline parallel to the cutting line. Measure from your hemline to the pattern's hemline and use this amount to lengthen or to shorten the garment. Mark the new hemline on the front and back pattern pieces.

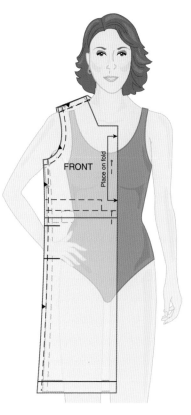

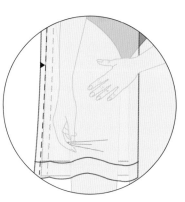

Walk pattern down; pinch at desired length.

Lengthening a Dress

1 On a worksheet, outline only the bottom cutting line and 1" along the side seam and the center front of the front pattern piece. Extend the grainline on the pattern; transfer it to the worksheet. Measure the needed amount **up** from the bottom cutting lines; mark.

> ◼ NOTE FROM NANCY
>
> *You may think I made a mistake when asking you to measure **up** to lengthen the pattern. The end result will add length, not take it away!*

2 Slide the pattern up, following the grainline to the increase mark.

3 Trace the rest of the pattern.

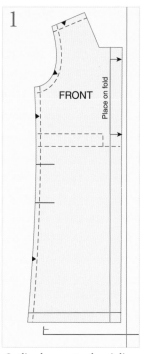

Outline hem; extend grainline; mark increase.

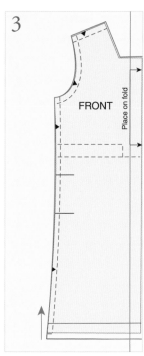

Slide pattern up; trace.

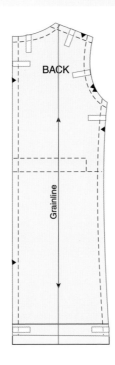

4 Without moving the pattern, tape it to the worksheet. Cut out the pattern, following the new outline.

5 Repeat steps 1 through 4 on the back pattern piece.

Shortening a Dress

1 Outline only the bottom cutting line and 1" along the side seam and the center front of the front pattern piece on a worksheet. Extend the grainline on the pattern; transfer it to the worksheet. Measure the needed amount **down** from the bottom cutting line; mark.

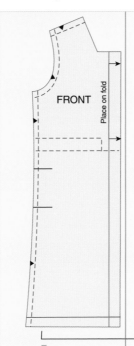

2 Slide the pattern down, following the grainline to the decrease mark.

3 Trace the rest of the pattern.

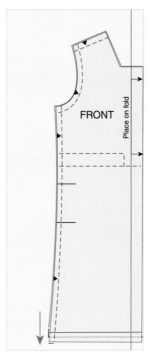

4 Without moving the pattern, tape it to the worksheet, folding up the pattern sections that overlap the new cutting line. Cut out the pattern, following the new outline.

5 Repeat steps 1 through 4 on the back pattern piece.

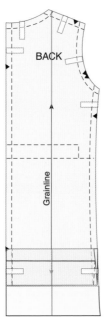

Sleeve Length Changes

Changing the Sleeve Length

Use the grainline as a guide to add sleeve length by sliding your pattern. If your Personal Fitting Chart indicates a change of ½" or more, lengthen or shorten the sleeve pattern.

	Pattern measurement	Body measurement	Change needed + or -
Bust	34"	36"	+2"
Waist	26-1/2"	25-1/2"	-1"
Hip	36"	39"	+3"
Back waist length	16-1/4"	16-1/2"	+1/2"
Upper arm	12"	12" + 1" = 13"	+1"
Sleeve length	22"	22-1/2""	+1/2"
Back width	18"	19"	+1-1/2"

Lengthening Sleeves

1 On a worksheet, outline only the lower edge of the sleeve pattern piece and 1" along each side seam.

2 Extend the grainline to the lower edge of the pattern; draw this extended grainline on the worksheet.

3 Measure the required amount up on the worksheet from the lower edge cutting line; mark.

4 Slide the pattern to trace the new cutting lines.
   - Slide the pattern up, following the grainline, until the lower edge meets the lengthening mark.

   - Trace the sleeve cap and the pattern sides, connecting the bottom to the original outline at the bottom edge.

5 Match the pattern to the outline on the worksheet. Fold up pattern sections that overlap the new cutting line; tape. Cut out the pattern, following the new outline.

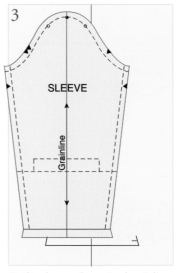

Outline lower edge; extend grainline.
Measure up; mark increase.

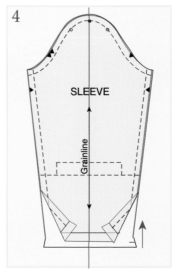

Slide pattern up; trace.

Completed adjustment

Shortening Sleeves

1 On a worksheet, outline only the lower edge of the sleeve pattern piece and 1" along each side seam.

2 Extend the grainline to the lower edge of the pattern; draw this extended grainline on the worksheet.

3 Measure down on the worksheet from the outlined lower edge the required amount; mark.

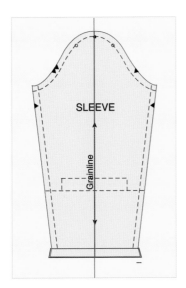

4 Slide the pattern down, following the grainline to the decrease mark. Trace the rest of the sleeve cap and taper the pattern sides to the sleeve hem.

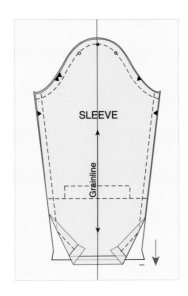

5 Without moving the pattern, tape it to the worksheet, folding up pattern sections that overlap the new cutting line. Cut out the shortened sleeve pattern piece, following the new outline.

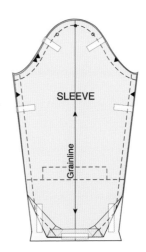

CHAPTER THREE

Combining
Fitting Techniques

Do you need fitting changes in more than one area? Be assured that you're not alone! This chapter is designed to assist you in making multiple fitting changes.

Combining Fitting Changes on One Worksheet

Up to this point, we've focused on individual changes. Since most of us may need two or more changes on our patterns, it's important to learn how to combine changes.

The *pattern fitting with confidence* approach allows you to make two or more changes on the same worksheet. To keep your changes accurate, follow a specific order for making the changes.

Front/Back Pattern Fitting Order

The order for fitting a blouse, top, jacket or dress is as follows:

1. Hem
2. Center (front or back)
3. Neckline
4. Shoulder
5. Armhole/Back width
6. Bust
7. Waist
8. Hip

Sleeve Pattern Fitting Order

The order is slightly different when fitting sleeves, since these pattern pieces do not have center fronts or backs. The sequence for modifying any type of sleeve is as follows:

1. Hem
2. Cap
3. Side seams

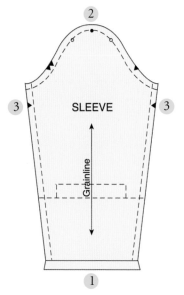

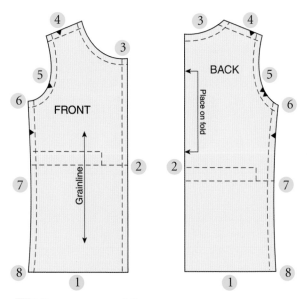

■ NOTE FROM NANCY

Looking at the illustrations, notice that on the front piece you work counterclockwise and on the back piece you work clockwise.

Increasing the Bustline and Hipline

It is very common to increase both the bustline and hipline in order to custom fit a pattern to your shape. Follow these basic instructions for easy and accurate results:

1 Outline the front and back pattern pieces on separate worksheets. Measure the needed increases for both the bustline and hipline; mark the worksheets.

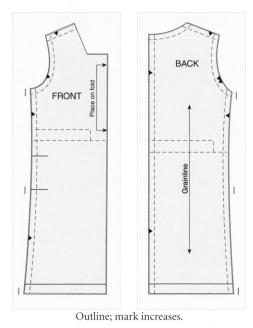

Outline; mark increases.

2   Work counterclockwise on the front piece, starting with the bustline increase allocation. (Work clockwise on the back piece.) Insert a pin at the stitching line where the shoulder and armhole intersect. Pivot the pattern to the bustline mark. Trace the new armhole cutting line.

3   Keep the pattern pivoted, and move the pin to where the armhole and side seam intersect. Pivot the pattern to the hipline mark. Trace the new side seam cutting line between the underarm and hipline.

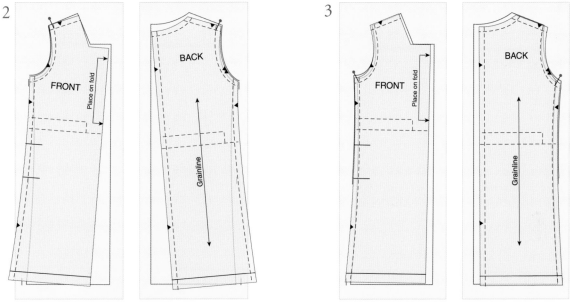

Pivot to increase mark; trace new armhole.   Pivot to increase mark; trace new side seam.

4   Keep the pattern pivoted, and move the pin to the hipline seam. Pivot the pattern to the mark at the hemline. Trace the new side seam between the hipline and hemline.

5   Match the pattern to the original outlines; tape. Cut out the pattern following the new outlines.

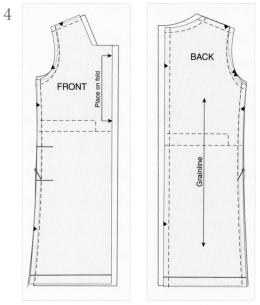

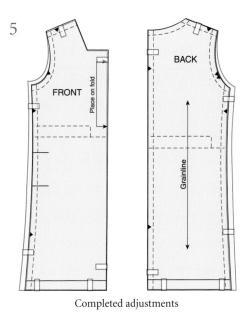

Pivot to increase mark; trace new side seam.   Completed adjustments

Combining Fitting Changes, continued

Increasing the Bustline and Decreasing the Hipline

Next let's try the combined change of increasing the bustline and decreasing the hipline. You'll notice that combining fitting changes—whether increasing or decreasing—follows the same process, making it possible to fit patterns with confidence!

1 Outline the front and back pattern pieces on separate worksheets. Measure the needed increase for the bustline and the needed decrease for the hipline; mark the worksheet.

2 Work counterclockwise on the front piece, starting with the bustline increase allocation. (Work clockwise on the back piece.) Insert a pin at the stitching line where the shoulder and armhole intersect. Pivot the pattern to the bustline increase. Trace the new armhole cutting line.

3 Keep the pattern pivoted, and move the pin to where the armhole and side seam intersect. Pivot the pattern to the hipline decrease. Trace the new side seam cutting line between the underarm and hipline.

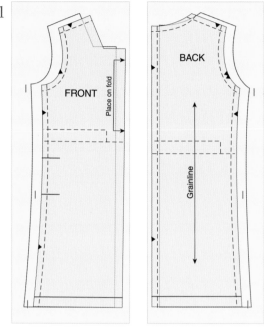

Outline; mark changes.

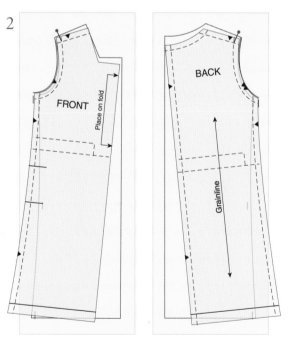

Pivot to increase mark; trace new armhole.

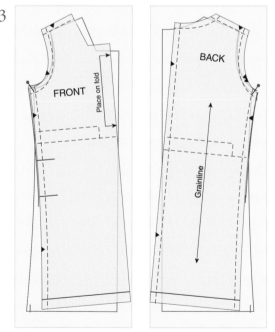

Pivot to decrease mark; trace new side seam.

4 Keep the pattern pivoted, and move the pin to the hipline seam. Pivot the pattern to the mark at the hemline. Trace the new side seam between the hipline and hemline.

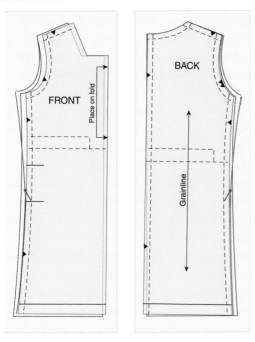

5 Match the pattern to the original outline. Tape and fold back the pattern at the hipline area. Cut out the pattern following the new outline.

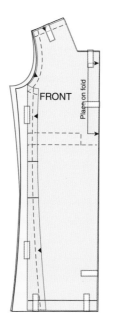

Typical Combined Fitting Changes

To help you visualize and practice how to combine pattern adjustments let's look at some typical fitting changes. The directions for each fitting change in this chapter are more generalized than in the preceding chapter. If you need to refresh your memory on the details of each change refer to the appropriate chapter.

Adjusting the Shoulder and the Bust

Adjusting for square shoulders and increasing the bust is a typical fitting change. I have abbreviated these directions. If you need more detailed instructions, refer to pages 20 and 35.

1 Outline the front pattern piece on the worksheet. Measure the needed changes for both fitting changes; mark the worksheet.

2 Work counterclockwise on the front pattern piece, starting with the square shoulder adjustment. (Work clockwise on the back pattern piece.) Insert a pin at the stitching line where the neck and shoulder intersect. Pivot the pattern to the square shoulder mark above the end of the shoulder seam. Trace the new shoulder cutting line.

3 Keep the pattern pivoted; move the pin to the stitching line where the shoulder and armhole intersect. Pivot the pattern to the bust increase mark. Trace the new armhole cutting line.

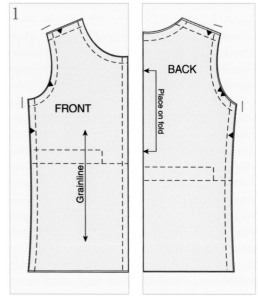

Outline; mark increases.

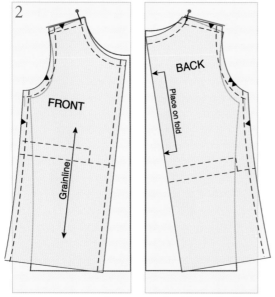

Pivot to increase mark; trace new shoulder cutting line.

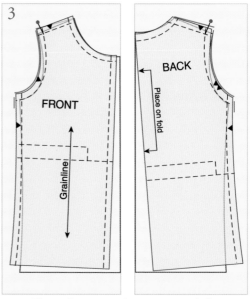

Pivot to increase mark; trace new armhole.

4 Keep the pattern pivoted; move the pin to the stitching line where the armhole and side seam intersect. Pivot the pattern to the original waist outline. Trace the cutting line between the underarm and the waist.

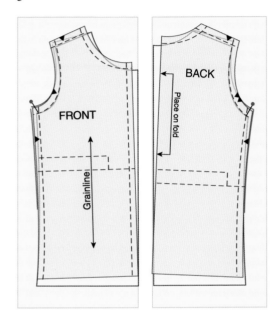

5 Match the pattern pieces to the original outlines; tape. Cut out the pattern, following the new outlines.

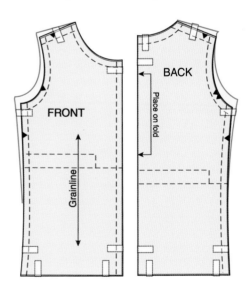

Increasing Sleeve Length and Width

It's easy to combine sleeve length and width changes on one worksheet. Let's practice!

1 Outline only the hem area of the sleeve pattern on the worksheet. Extend the grainline. Measure up the needed length increase from the bottom; mark.

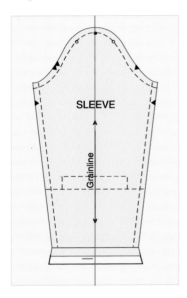

2 Slide the pattern up, following the grainline to the increase mark. Trace the rest of the pattern.

3 Measure out the needed increase on each side of the underarm; mark.

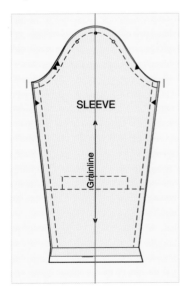

4 Place a pin at the large dot on the stitching line at the cap of the sleeve. Pivot to the increase mark at one of the side seams. Trace half the cap and 1" around the corner of the sleeve.

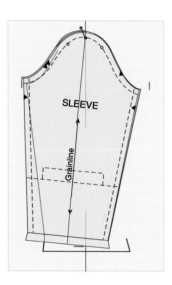

5 Keep the pattern pivoted; move the pin to the stitching line where the sleeve cap and the side seam intersect. Pivot the pattern to the side cutting line near the hem. Trace the new side cutting line.

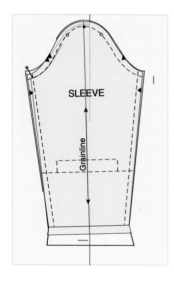

6 Move the pattern to its original position in step 3. Repeat steps 4 and 5 on the other half of the sleeve. Tape the pattern to the worksheet, matching the cap areas. Cut out the pattern, following the new outline.

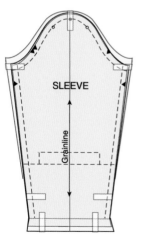

Adjusting Back, Bustline and Hipline

Three or more fitting changes can be incorporated on one worksheet. Just remember to follow the pattern fitting order, page 48. This example incorporates increasing the bustline and hipline, plus lengthening the back.

1 Outline the front and back pattern pieces. Measure the additional length needed on the back piece; mark. Measure out the needed increase at the bust and hip; mark.

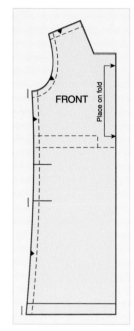
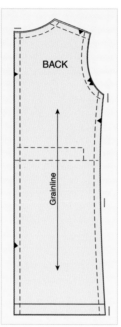

2 Slide the back pattern piece up to the mark above the neckline. Trace the neck cutting line.

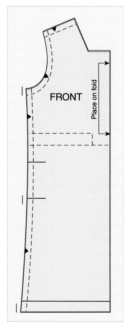
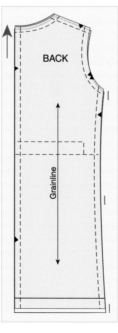

3 Place a pin at the stitching line where the neck and shoulder intersect. Pivot to the original outline at the armhole. Trace the shoulder cutting line.

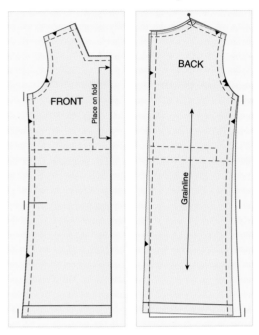

4 Place a pin at the stitching line where the shoulder and armhole intersect. Pivot the pattern to meet the bustline increase mark. Trace the new armhole cutting line.

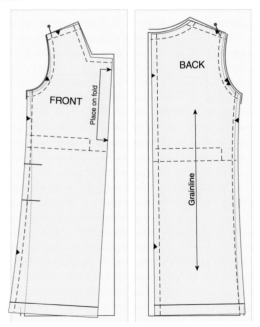

Typical Combined Fitting Changes, *continued*

5   Keep the pattern pivoted. Move the pin to where the armhole and side seam intersect. Pivot the pattern to the hipline mark. Trace the new side seam cutting line between the underarm and hipline.

6   Keep the pattern pivoted. Move the pin to the hipline seam. Pivot the pattern to the mark at the hemline. Trace the new side seam between the hipline and hemline.

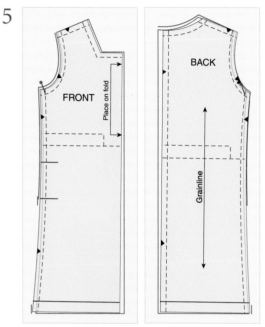

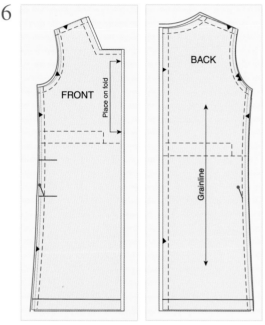

Move pin to where armhole and side seam intersect; pivot to hipline mark; trace new cutting line between armhole and hipline.

Move pin to hipline seam; pivot to mark at hemline; trace remainder of side seam.

7   Match the pattern to the original outlines; tape. Cut out the pattern following the new outlines.

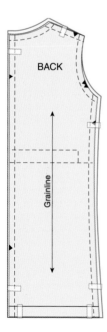

Adding Extensions

If you need to add more than 1" per side seam at the bust or to the sleeve width, fine-tune the fit with extensions—sections added in equal amounts to the bust and to the sleeve. Extensions are added in tandem with pivoting increases. This system ensures that your armhole seams match and that your finished garment fits well and hangs nicely.

▮ NOTE FROM NANCY

The limit of pivoting 1" per side seam applies only to the bust and the sleeve. Pivoting techniques can increase the hip and the waist by any amount—there's no limit.

When using extensions, it is important that you make **both** the sleeve and bust changes outlined below.

Determining Sleeve Changes

If your *Personal Fitting Chart* on page 122 indicates that you need to add more than 4" at the bust or more than 2" at the sleeve, make the sleeve changes first. Subtract the maximum amount allowed for sleeve pivoting (2") from the amount you need to add. The remainder will become extensions. For example:

Sleeve increase	4"
Maximum pivoting	-2"
(1" per side seam)	
Needed extensions	+2"

(or 1" per side seam)

You will have to add the same extensions to the bust area so that your sleeve armholes match your garment armholes. Use this extension amount to determine the needed bust increase.

Determining Bust Changes

For the sleeve to match the garment's underarm, the extension must be the same size at both the sleeve and the bust. Subtract the sleeve extension amount from the bust increase to determine how much to pivot. For example:

Bust increase	5"
Extension	-4"
(same as for sleeves)	
Pivoting	+1"

(or ¼" per side seam)

Adding Bust and Sleeve Extensions

1. Outline the sleeve pattern piece and the garment front and back pattern pieces on worksheets.

2. Pivot the sleeve pattern piece as shown on pages 29–31 and the bust pattern piece as shown on page 20. For the example, you would pivot 1" per side seam for the sleeve and ¼" per side seam for the bust.

3. Add extensions to the sleeve.
   - Measure out 1" from the new cutting line at the underarm.
   - Slide the sleeve pattern piece to the increase mark; trace the extension from the end of the pivot increase to the corner.
   - On short sleeves, add the extensions the entire length of the side seam.

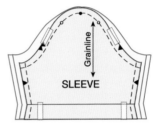

   - On long sleeves, taper the extensions to the elbow area (middle of the underarm cutting line).

4. Add an extension to the bodice. For the example, you would measure out 1" from the new cutting line at the underarm of the front and back pattern pieces. Taper the extension to the cutting line at the waist.

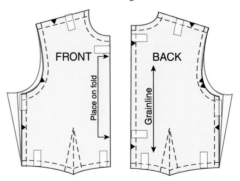

5. Match the pattern pieces to the original outlines; tape. Cut out the pattern, following the new outlines.

▮ NOTE FROM NANCY

You must always use pivoting in combination with extensions. Without the adjustments pivoting provides, an extension does not give the room you need to raise your arm.

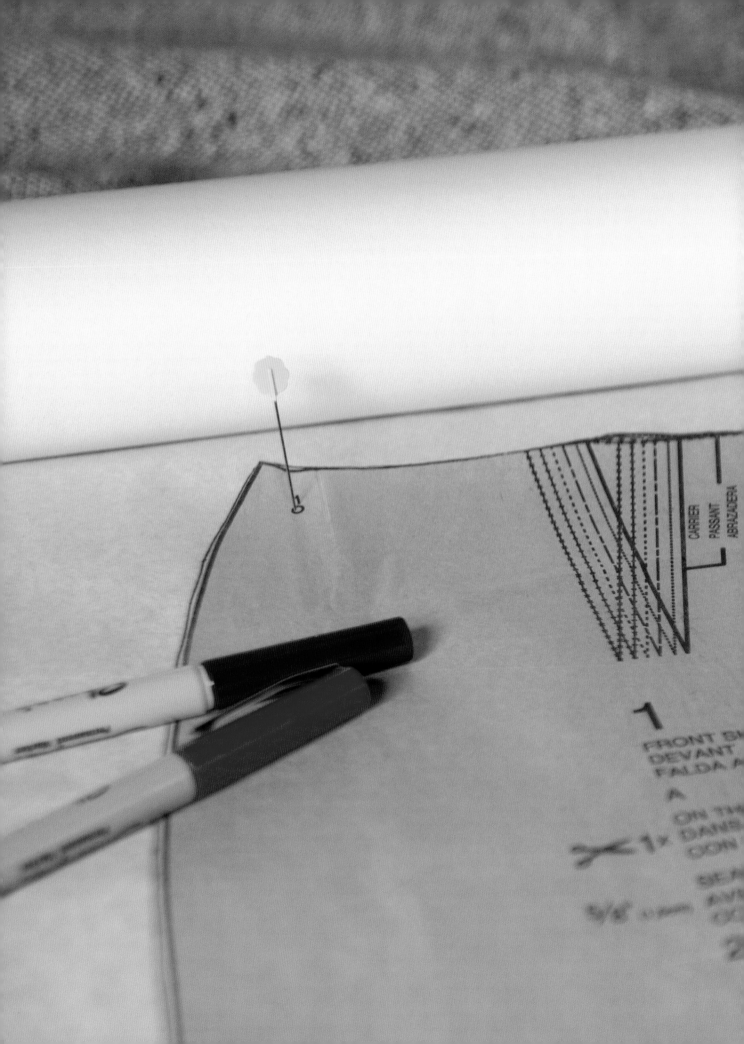

CARRIER
PASSANT
ABRAZADERA

1
FRONT S
DEVANT
FALDA A
A
ON TH
1x DANS
CON
5/8" AV

CHAPTER FOUR

Fitting Skirts

With a little fitting confidence and two key measurements— the waist and the hip— a perfect fitting skirt becomes a reality! Skirt fitting changes included for the waist, hip, and length are fast and easy.

Waist Changes

Pattern Sizing

Purchase your skirt pattern by either the waist or hip measurement. If you fall between sizes, take your choice!

If the pattern includes several garment components (jacket, blouse, skirt, and pants), purchase the size according to your Right Size Measurement, see page 9, since fitting a garment above the waist requires specific sizing.

Hipline Reference

Mark a hipline directly on the pattern. Measure down from the waistline on the pattern piece the amount of your hipline length. (See page 11 for how to take this measurement.) Draw this reference line directly on the skirt front and back pattern pieces, at right angles (perpendicular to) the grainline.

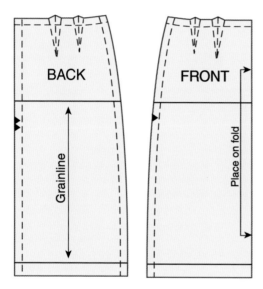

Fast Waist Changes

An easy slide and pivot of the pattern can quickly add or subtract inches from the pattern waistline. Make these changes at the side seams to maintain the grainline and the style of the pattern.

Determining Changes

If your Personal Fitting Chart indicates a change of more than ½" divide the fitting change by four, the number of cut edges at both side seams. In the example, add ½" to each cut edge.

	Pattern measurement	Body measurement	Change needed + or -
Bust	34"	34-1/2"	+1/2"
Waist	26-1/2"	28-1/2"	+2"
Hip	36"	37"	+1"
Back waist length	16-1/4"	16-1/4"	0
Upper arm	12"	12" + 1" = 13"	+1"
Sleeve length	22"	21"	-1"
Back width	18"	19"	+1"

Increasing

1   Outline the front pattern piece on a worksheet. Measure out from the waist for the increase; mark.

2   Slide the pattern to the mark; trace the wider waist.

3   Place a pin at the stitching lines where the waistline and side seams intersect. Pivot the pattern in to the original outline at the hip. Trace the new cutting line between the waist and the hip.

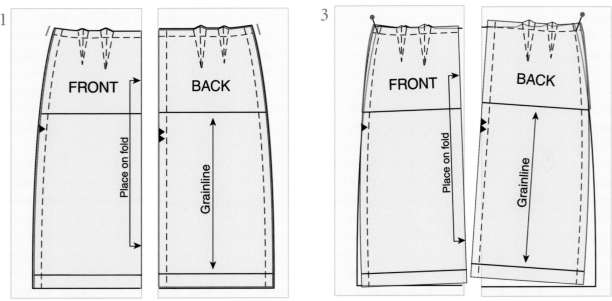

Outline pattern; mark increase.   Pivot and trace new hip outline.

4   Match the pattern to the original outline; tape. Cut out the pattern, following the new outline.

5   Repeat steps 1 through 4 on the back pattern piece. Adjust the waistband accordingly. (See *Adjusting the Waistband*, pages 62–63.)

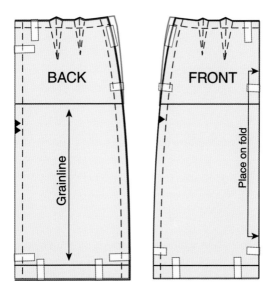

Waist and Waistband Changes

Decreasing

1 Outline the front pattern piece on a worksheet. Measure in at the waist for the decrease amount; mark.

2 Slide the pattern to the mark.

3 Place a pin at the stitching line where the waistline and side seam intersect; pivot the pattern out to the original outline at the hip. Trace the new cutting line between the waist and the hip.

4 Match the pattern to the original outline; tape. Fold in the pattern sections that overlap the new outline. Cut out the pattern, following the new outline.

5 Repeat steps 1 through 4 on the back pattern piece. Adjust the waistband accordingly.

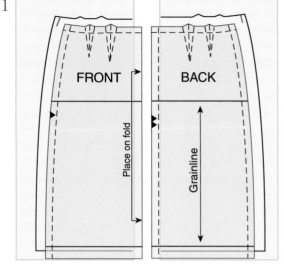

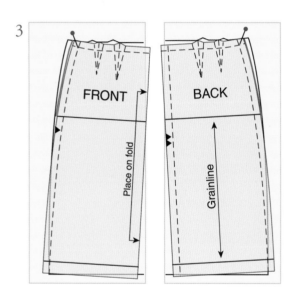

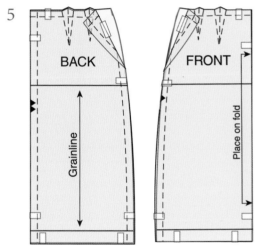

Adjusting the Waistband

Changing a waistband is the simplest of all fitting techniques, but transferring the markings has been another story—until now.

Increasing

1 Outline the waistband pattern piece on a worksheet; mark the increase to correspond to the amount added to the skirt waist.

2 Slide the pattern to the mark; trace the new cutting lines. Cut out the pattern, following the new outline.

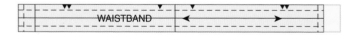

3 Place a length of elastic longer than the original waistband pattern piece along the notched lengthwise edge of the pattern. Match one end of the elastic to one pattern end; mark the opposite pattern end on the elastic.

▌ NOTE FROM NANCY
It's not necessary to cut the elastic to a particular size as long as it's longer than your waistband. Since you only need it for the markings, use a length from your sewing basket. When you're done, you can still use it for sewing.

4 Transfer pattern markings (single and double notches, center front, circles, and squares) to the elastic with a marking pen.

5 Stretch the elastic so that the pattern end markings match the worksheet; secure the elastic to the worksheet. Transfer the markings to the worksheet. This proportionally increases the pattern markings to fit the adjusted waistband.

■ **NOTE FROM NANCY**

It helps to have three hands to carry out this quick fitting change! If your sewing buddy isn't available, pin both the pattern and the elastic to a firm padded surface to anchor the stretched elastic while you transfer the markings.

Decreasing

Elastic is the key to marking a smaller waistband as well. Just reverse the order of the steps you used to mark an increased waistband.

1 Outline the waistband pattern piece on a worksheet. Mark the decrease to correspond to the amount subtracted from the waist.

2 Slide pattern to the mark; trace the new cutting lines. Cut out the pattern, following the new outline.

3 Fold back one end of the original waistband pattern piece the amount decreased from the waistband. Place a length of elastic longer than the original waistband pattern piece along the notched edge of the worksheet.

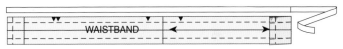

Mark decreased size of elastic.

4 Unfold the pattern to its original size; match the end of the elastic to one end of the pattern. Stretch the elastic to the original pattern size; trace the pattern markings (single and double notches, center front, circles, and squares) onto the elastic with a marking pen.

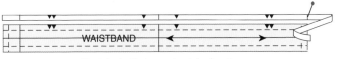

Stretch elastic to meet original pattern; transfer markings..

5 Release the elastic, match the end markings to the worksheet, and secure it to the worksheet. Transfer the markings from the elastic to the worksheet.

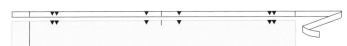

Transfer markings to worksheet.

Hip Changes

Hip changes are among the most common fitting changes made. To maintain the style of the pattern, add or subtract the same amount at the hip and the hem.

Determining Changes

If your Personal Fitting Chart indicates a change of more than ½", divide the fitting change by four, the number of cut edges at both side seams. In the example below, add 1" to each side of both the front and back pattern pieces.

	Pattern measurement	Body measurement	Change needed + or -
Bust	34"	34-1/2"	+1/2"
Waist	26-1/2"	28-1/2"	+2"
Hip	36"	40"	+4"
Back waist length	16-1/4"	16-1/4"	0

Increasing

1 Outline the pattern on a worksheet. Measure the needed increase out from both the hip cutting line and the hem cutting line; mark.

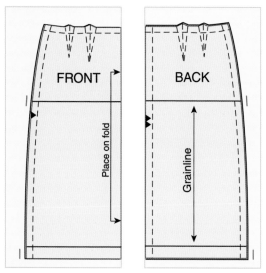

2 Place a pin at the stitching lines where the waistline and side seams intersect. Pivot the pattern out to the increase mark at the hip. Trace the new cutting line between the waist and the hip.

3 Keeping the pattern pivoted, move the pin to the stitching line at the hipline. Pivot the pattern to the increase mark at the hem. Trace the new cutting line between the hip and the hem.

4 Match the pattern to the original outline. Tape it to the worksheet. Cut out the pattern, following the new outline.

5 Repeat steps 1 through 4 on the back pattern piece.

2

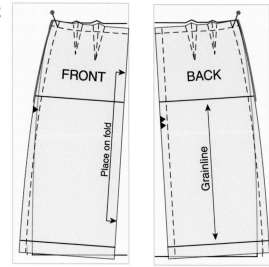

Pivot to increase mark; trace new cutting line.

3

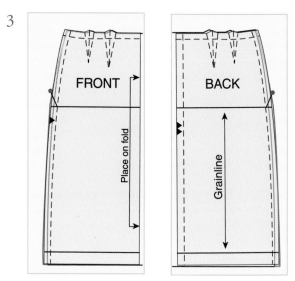

Pivot to increase mark; trace new cutting line.

5

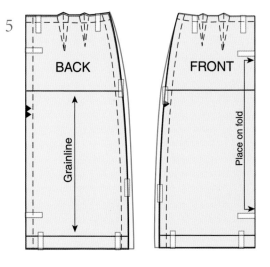

Decreasing

1 Outline the pattern on a worksheet. Measure the needed decrease in from both the hip cutting line and the hem cutting line; mark.

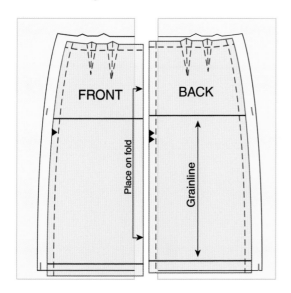

2 Place a pin at the stitching lines where the waistline and side seams intersect. Pivot the pattern in to the decrease mark at the hip. Trace the new cutting line between the waist and the hip.

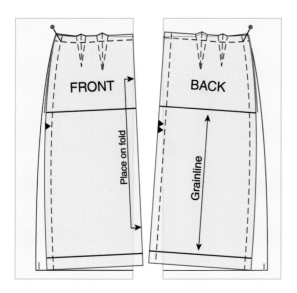

3 Keeping the pattern pivoted, move the pin to the stitching line at the hipline. Pivot the pattern to the decrease mark at the hem. Trace the new cutting line between the hip and the hem.

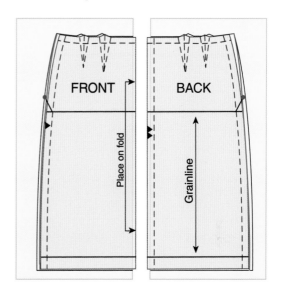

4 Match the pattern to the original outline; tape it to the worksheet. Fold in the pattern sections that overlap the new outline. Cut out the pattern, following the new outline.

5 Repeat steps 1 through 4 on the back pattern piece.

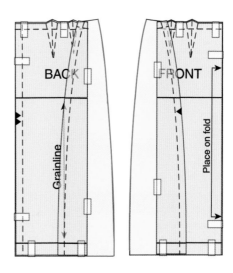

Fitting for a High Hip

If you have one hip that is slightly higher than the other, the fabric of your skirts most likely pulls with diagonal stress wrinkles on the higher side, resulting in an uneven hem. If you have a high hip, avoid plaids and stripes, which accentuate the changes made to fit the garment.

◼ NOTE FROM NANCY

It is fairly common to have one high hip on the side opposite one square shoulder. See Square Shoulders *on page 35.*

1 Outline the front pattern piece on the worksheet.

2 Use a fashion ruler to add shape between the original waist and the hip, creating a more predominant curve; redraw the side seam cutting line.

3 Adjust the back pattern piece following the same steps.

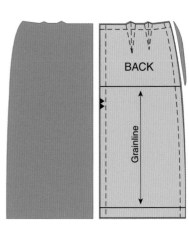

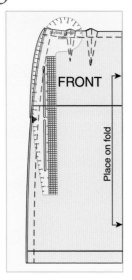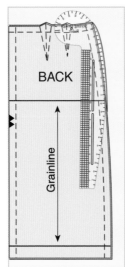

4 Match the pattern to the original outline; tape. Cut out the pattern, following the new outline. Cut out the skirt. Untape the pattern from the worksheet.

5 Trim the excess fabric from the lower hip side.

- On the **right** (not wrong) side of your fabric, mark the side that corresponds to your high hip (right or left).
- Place the pattern on the side of the skirt fabric that does **not** accommodate the high hip. Double-check to be sure you mark the correct side.
- Trim the excess fabric from the lower hip side on both the front and back pieces.

◼ NOTE FROM NANCY

The fitting change in step 2 affects both side seams. I find if easier and faster to cut both sides of a skirt with the high hip fitting change; then trim the excess fabric from the lower hip side.

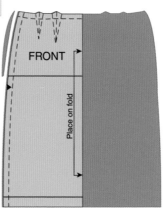

◼ NOTE FROM NANCY

"High hip" most often refers to having one side higher than the other. But if your figure is full above both hips and below the waist, this is also called "high hip." To fit a skirt with both high hips, follow steps 1 through 4 for Fitting for a High Hip. *In this instance, do not trim away any fabric. This provides the fitting change you need for both sides.*

Hem Changes

Use the slide technique to add or subtract length to a skirt pattern. Extend the grainline (see page 42) and use this as a guideline when sliding your pattern up or down.

NOTE FROM NANCY

The advantages of changing the skirt length by sliding the pattern are that it keeps the pattern intact and the shape at the side seams remains even. It may seem faster and easier just to cut the pattern longer or shorter, but generally that super-quick method is not as accurate.

Determining Changes

Compare the pattern length to your figure.
- Pin the natural waist of the front pattern to the waist of your undergarment. Align the center front of the pattern with your undergarment's center front; pin.
- Walk the skirt pattern piece down your figure, pinch the pattern at the desired length, and mark it with a pencil. Unpin the pattern.
- Add hem allowance as indicated on the pattern, drawing the hemline parallel to the bottom cutting line. Measure from your hemline to the pattern's hemline. This is the amount to lengthen or to shorten the skirt.

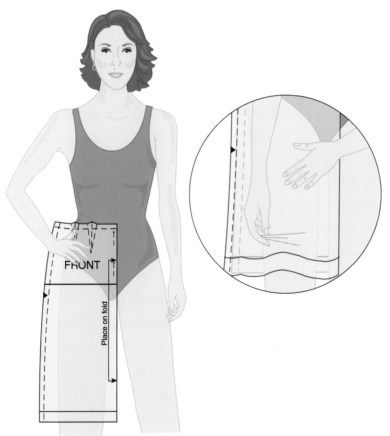

Hem Changes, continued

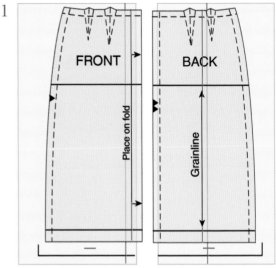

Outline bottom and 1" along side seam; mark hem change.

Lengthening

1. Extend the grainline the full length of the pattern. On a worksheet, outline only the bottom cutting line and 1" along the side seam of the skirt front pattern piece. Measure the needed fitting change up from the bottom cutting line; mark.

2. Slide the pattern up to the mark, aligning the grainline.

3. Trace the rest of the side cutting line, the waist, and the center front.

4. Without moving the pattern, tape it to the worksheet. Cut out the pattern, following the new outline.

5. Repeat steps 1 through 4 on the back pattern piece.

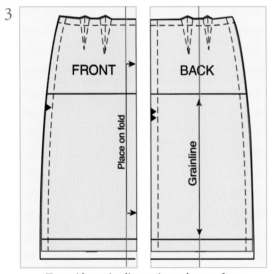

Trace side cutting line, waist, and center front.

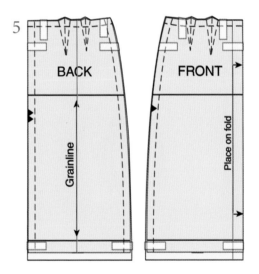

Shortening

1. Outline the pattern and mark the decrease.
   - On a worksheet, outline only the bottom cutting line and 1" along the side seam of the front pattern piece.
   - Measure down from the bottom cutting line the amount needed to shorten the pattern; mark.

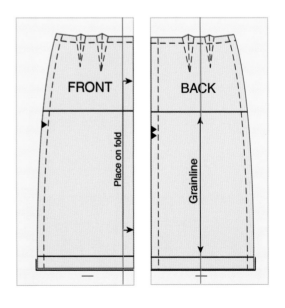

2 Slide the pattern down to the mark, aligning the grainline.

3 Trace the rest of the side cutting line, the waist, and the center front.

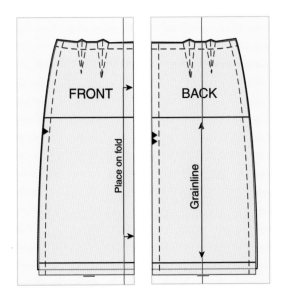

4 Without moving the pattern, tape it to the worksheet. Fold in the pattern sections that overlap the new outline. Cut out the pattern, following the new outline.

5 Repeat steps 1 through 4 on the back pattern piece.

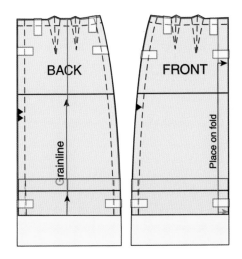

NOTE FROM NANCY

On a gored, flared or A-line skirt, taper the side seam to meet the width outlined at the hem. This step will keep the hem the same width as the pattern designer intended.

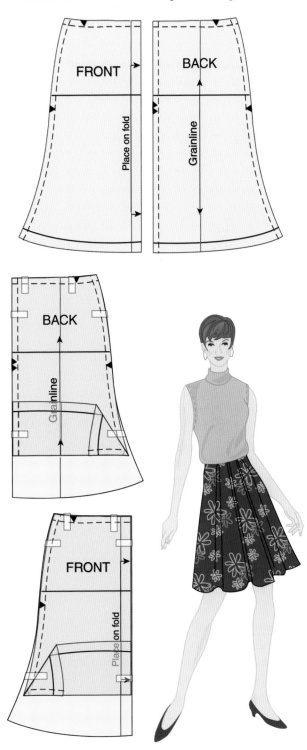

Combining Fitting Changes

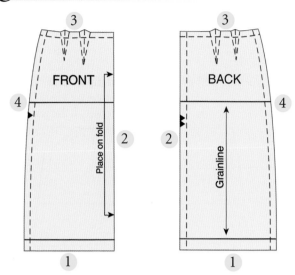

Sometimes you may need more than one fitting change on a skirt pattern. You have two options: Make each fitting change on a separate worksheet and then tape them together, or take a streamlined approach and do all changes on one worksheet.

Here's the easy one worksheet approach and the order to follow when making fitting changes to a skirt. The sequence naturally flows around the pattern, keeping the pattern's grainline on target. Follow the sequence listed below.

Front/Back Pattern Fitting Order

1. Hem

2. Center (front or back)

3. Waistline

4. Side seam

■ **NOTE FROM NANCY**
Notice on the front piece you'll be working counter-clockwise and on the back piece, clockwise.

One Worksheet Approach

1 Hem—Hem changes should be the first priority with a one worksheet approach. Outline the hem, and then slide the pattern up or down to shorten or to lengthen the pattern. After changing the length, outline the remaining cutting lines and mark all the needed changes on the worksheet.

2 Center—If you have a swayback fitting change, make that change next on the skirt pattern.

■ **NOTE FROM NANCY**
A swayback cannot be measured, page 41; it's only vis-ible during the fine-tuning stage of fitting. If you find and correct for a swayback, on future skirt projects you can incorporate the change as needed when you make other fitting changes.

3 Waist—The third sequence is the waist area. If you need to increase or decrease the waist or to adjust for a high hip, make these changes next.

4 Hip—The last area to adjust when combining changes on one worksheet is the hip area.

Lengthening Skirt and Increasing Waist and Hip

1 Extend the grainline the full length of the pattern. Outline the pattern and mark the hem change.
- Outline only the bottom cutting line of the front pattern and 1" along the side seam on a worksheet.
- To lengthen the pattern, measure the needed fitting change up from the bottom cutting line; mark.

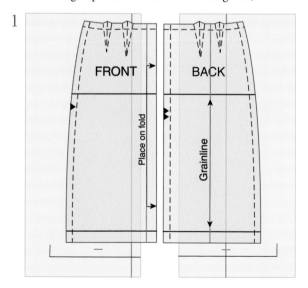

2 Slide the pattern up to the mark, aligning the grainline. Trace the waist and the side cutting lines on the worksheet.

3 Make increases at both the hip and the waist.
   • Measure and mark the needed waist increase.
   • Measure and mark the needed hip increase at both the hip and the hem.
   • Slide the pattern to the waist increase mark. Trace the waist.
   • Place a pin at the stitching line where the waistline and side seams intersect. Pivot the pattern to the hip increase mark. Trace the new cutting line between the waist and the hip.

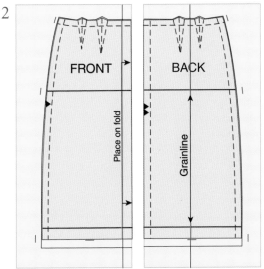

Trace waist and side cutting lines; mark increase.

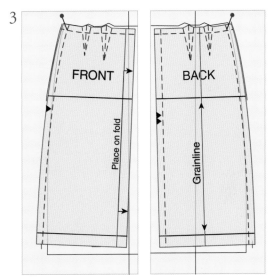

Pivot to hip increase mark, trace new cutting line.

4 Keeping the pattern pivoted, move the pin to the stitching line at the hipline. Pivot to the mark at the hem. Trace the new cutting line between the hip and the hem.

5 Match the pattern to the original outline; tape. Cut out the pattern, following the new outline. Repeat steps 1 through 4 on the back pattern piece.

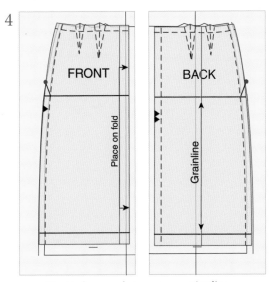

Pivot to hem mark, trace new cutting line.

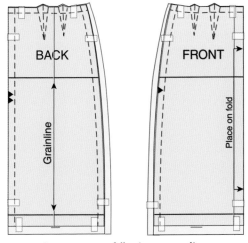

Cut out pattern following new outlines.

CHAPTER FIVE

Fitting Pants

Pants fitting is always popular! Meet the challenge using these easy fitting techniques. Learn to choose the correct size, measure your figure, measure the pattern pieces, and fit the pattern. Stylish pants with fitted comfort are so rewarding!

Determining Size

The traditional guideline for pants has been to buy the pattern according to your hip measurement. However, when this measurement is used to choose a size, too often the hip of the pants may fit properly, but the legs bag like pajamas, and the crotch hangs too low.

An easy solution is to choose a smaller pattern size and adjust it to fit the hip. Remember: It is much easier to enlarge a pattern than to reduce it. A smaller pattern size keeps the legs and crotch proportional.

Measuring to Determine Size

To fit pant patterns with confidence, choose a pattern according to the Pant Pattern Size Chart, page 123. Most likely, you'll buy a smaller pattern size than you have in the past and then adjust it to enlarge the hip.

- Measure the fullest part of your hips, making sure that the tape measure is parallel with the floor.

- Refer to the *Pant Pattern Size Chart*, page 123, to determine which size to purchase.
- Buy a classic-style pattern without stylized pockets or yokes.

▌ NOTE FROM NANCY

The Pant Pattern Size Chart *has two benefits: Choosing the smaller size eliminates the baggy fit in the legs and the low-hanging crotch. Plus, fitting into a smaller size is a real ego booster!*

The hip fits but nothing else does.

Additional Sizing Guidelines

- If your hip measurement falls between sizes and your thighs are proportional to your hip, choose the size closest to your hip measurement. If your thighs are slender compared to your hip, choose the smaller size. If your thighs are heavier, use the larger size.
- If your hip measurement is greater than 50", use the Misses' size 22 pattern.

▌ NOTE FROM NANCY

I never recommend using a pattern larger than a size 22, because larger pattern sizes create pant legs that are uncontrollably baggy. It's much easier to make the hip area larger than it is to make all other areas smaller.

Measuring Your Figure

The next step to fitting pants with finesse is to take six measurements. Three of these are length measurements—pant length, side curve and crotch; three are width measurements—waist, hip and thigh. To achieve a great fit, you must measure and compare the first five of these with the pattern measurements. The thigh measurement is only necessary if the widest part of your figure is in the thigh area. For convenience record all of these measurements on your *Personal Fitting Chart for Pants*, page 123.

Pant Length

■ NOTE FROM NANCY

For best results, recruit your sewing buddy to help take these measurements. Work as a team so that you can both make pants that fit.

To make it easy to figure out where to stop and start measuring pant length, wear a pair of pants that are a comfortable length. Have your sewing buddy measure the side seam from your "shelf" (below the waist but above the hipbone, where the waist seam of your pants actually rests) to the finished length.

Side Curve Length

Most of us are concerned with the number of inches around our figure, but the hip's shape and curve are also extremely important. A high, curvy hip needs more side length than usual. A low, flat hip needs less.

■ NOTE FROM NANCY

If you've ever noticed that the crease on one pant leg hangs straight and the other bows out, it's caused by one hip being higher than the other—a very common figure trait!

The side length affects the way creases hang. If the side seam is too long, creases hang inward. If it's too short, creases bow out.

Side seam too long makes crease bow in.

Side seam too short makes crease bow out.

Determining Size, *continued*

The side curve length is measured from the shelf to the crotchline. To measure the side curve:

- Stitch an elastic strip in a circle and place it around your leg to show your crotchline (or wear a pair of brief-style panties and use the leg elastic on them).
- Slide your thumb down your side from the waist until it rests on your shelf (above the hip but below the waist, where the waist seam of a comfortable pair of pants rests).
- Measure to the closest 1" from your shelf to your panty line.
- Repeat this procedure on the other side; record both measurements.

> ▌ NOTE FROM NANCY
> *Measure both side curve lengths. If there is a difference, use the longer measurement.*

Crotch Length

For most people, fitting the crotch presents the biggest challenge to making pants that fit well. If the crotch length is too short, wrinkles radiate from the seat area. If the length is too long, the crotch hangs too low. In either case, the pants are uncomfortable to wear.

Crotch length that is too short causes wrinkles under the seat (left); crotch length that is too long causes wrinkles in front (right).

Fitting the crotch is a two-step process, and you'll learn both steps in this chapter. The first step is to measure your figure using the instructions below. Then read on to determine where to make changes.

To measure the crotch length:

- Use the same shelf that you used to measure the pant and side curve lengths. Those two measurements were taken from the side shelf, and the crotch length is taken from the same area below your waist at center front and back.
- Place one end of the tape measure at the front shelf and run the tape between your legs; stop at the back shelf (generally, the deepest part of the sway in your back). Take this measurement exactly the way you want your pants to fit, not too tight or too loose; record.

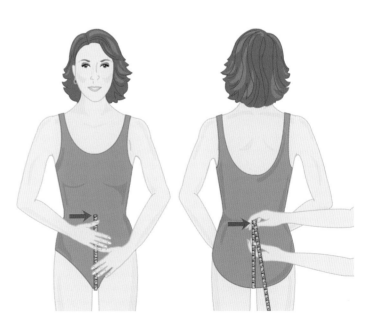

Adding Ease

Pant patterns vary a great deal in their actual width measurements. One designer may allow more room in the seat than others, while another styles the pants wider in the thighs or the waist. Because of this variety, you'll need to compare your body width measurements to width measurements you take from the pant pattern.

Pattern widths always include ease (extra inches for comfort and style). As part of the *pattern fitting with confidence* method, you add a specific amount of ease to each body width measurement before recording it on the *Personal Fitting Chart for Pants* so that comparisons to pattern widths will be accurate.

Waist

- To take this measurement, first bend to the side; the deepest resulting wrinkle is your waist.

Stand straight again and measure around your waist, keeping the tape measure parallel to the floor. Place a thumb or a finger underneath the tape measure to prevent the measurement from being taken too tightly. Measure to the closest ½".
- Add 1" of ease to this measurement before recording it.

Hip

- Measure the fullest part of the hip, keeping the tape measure parallel to the floor and your finger underneath the tape to make sure it is not too tight. Measure to the closest ½".

- Add 2" of ease to this measurement before recording it.

Thigh

It is only necessary to measure your thigh if the widest part of your figure is in the thigh area.
- Measure the fullest part of either upper leg.

- Add 1" of ease to this measurement before recording it.

Measuring the Pattern

Preparing Pant Patterns

Pattern fitting with confidence for pants relies on simple pivot and slide techniques for pattern fitting changes. This five-step process allows you to custom-fit clothes using worksheets made of inexpensive wax paper, pattern paper, or tissue paper. To make your pattern larger or smaller, pivot the pattern like a pendulum, inserting a straight pin at a key point. Or, slide the pattern. Your original pattern remains intact.

Detailed instructions for using pivot and slide techniques are given on page 17.

Drawing Reference Lines

When instructions call for adding a reference line or extending the grainline, use a yardstick and a marking pen to draw on the pattern.

Transfer the line to the worksheet by using a tracing wheel. Place the pattern on top of the worksheet; trace along the line. The tracing wheel points will perforate the worksheet, producing a guideline.

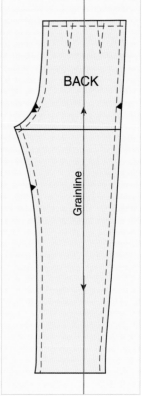

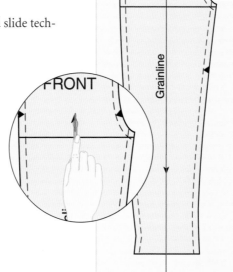

Grainlines

Extend the grainline the full length of the pattern and the worksheet to make it easier to slide the pattern up and down when changing length.

Reference Lines

Draw reference lines perpendicular to the grainline printed on the pattern.

For a crotchline, use the point where the crotch and inseam stitching lines intersect to position the line.

For a hipline, measure 2" above the crotchline.

For a kneeline, locate the point midway between the crotchline and the hemline.

> ■ **NOTE FROM NANCY**
> *You've probably never been asked to find the kneeline of a pattern before! Rest assured, you're not going to fit the pattern at the knee. You will only use that area as a pivot point. To find the kneeline easily, fold the pattern up, meeting the hem to the crotchline. The fold will indicate the kneeline.*

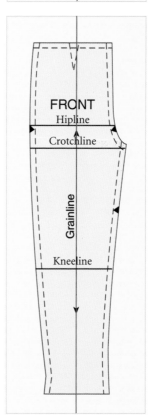

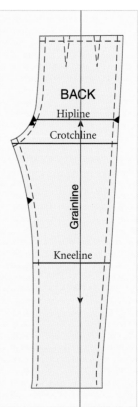

Measuring the Pattern

In earlier chapters, we used the ease allowed in the pattern and simply compared our measurements to the measurements written on the back of the pattern envelope. But with pants, my experience shows it is worth the extra step of comparing your measurements (including ease) to the actual pattern measurements. This more specific plan will build your confidence and give great results! Record the pattern measurements and adjustment amounts on the *Personal Fitting Chart for Pants*, page 123.

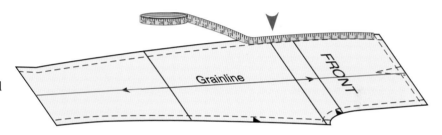

■ **NOTE FROM NANCY**

It's important to measure the pattern's side curve first and then, with the tape measure in the same place, check the pattern pant length. Both of these measurements are taken on the side and work in tandem to give you the best fit along the outer side seam.

Pattern Side Curve

- Use the front pattern piece for this measurement.
- Find your side curve measurement on the tape measure. Hold this point on the tape measure to the pattern at the crotchline along the side seam.

■ **NOTE FROM NANCY**

The crotchline should be printed on the front pattern piece. If not, simply draw a line perpendicular to the grainline from the crotch point to the side seam.

- If the tape measure ends below the waist stitching line, position the other end of the tape measure so that the tab ends meet. Read the amount shown on the tape at the stitching line; record.

- If the tape measure extends above the waist stitching line, read the measurement at the waist stitching line; record.

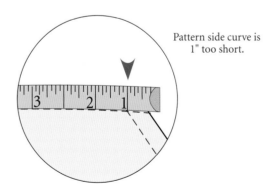

Pattern side curve is ⅜" too long.

Pattern side curve is 1" too short.

■ **NOTE FROM NANCY**

Don't worry about additions or subtractions that are less than ¼". I always weigh more on Mondays than on Fridays, yet my clothes still fit!

Pattern Pant Length

- Keep the tape measure held to the crotchline at your side curve measurement.

- Add the hem allowance amount from the pattern to the pant length measurement from the *Personal Fitting Chart for Pants*, page 123, to give you the cutting line of the hem. For example, if the pattern allows a 1½" hem, add 1½" to your pant length recorded on the chart.

- To measure the difference between the cutting line of the hem on the pattern and your measurement, position the tape measure flat and extend it to the cutting line of the pattern piece.

- If the measurement for your cutting line is above the pattern cutting line, position the other end of the tape measure so that the tab end meets the amount for your cutting line. Read the measurement at the cutting line; record.

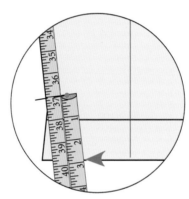

- If the measurement for your cutting line is below the pattern cutting line, position the other end of the tape measure so that the tab end meets the pattern cutting line. Read the measurement at the marked length; record.

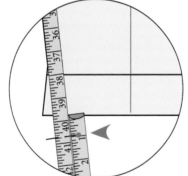

Pattern Crotch Length

- Pin the crotch points together, stacking stitching lines.

- Place the end of the tape measure at the center back waist stitching line. Stand the tape measure on edge and place it around the curved stitching line to the center front waist stitching line; record.

- Compare your crotch measurement with the pattern crotch measurement to determine if a fitting change is necessary.

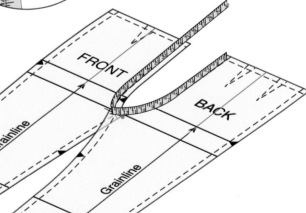

Pattern Waist—for a fitted waistline

- Fold the darts of the pattern closed at the waist seam.
- Pin the front and back pattern pieces together at the side seam, stacking stitching lines at the waist.
- Measure along the waist seam between stitching lines, standing the tape measure on its side. Double the measurement to achieve the actual width; record.

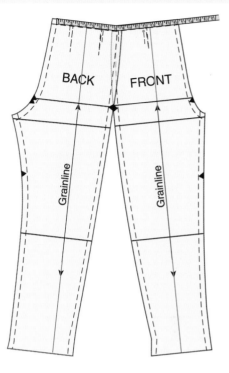

> ■ NOTE FROM NANCY
>
> *A tape measure can serve as a quick calculator. To double a measurement, fold the tape at the measured mark. The end of the tape will be at the doubled amount.*

- Compare your waist measurement with the pattern waist measurement to determine if you need to make an adjustment.

Pattern Hip

- Pin the pattern pieces together at the side seam, stacking stitching lines at the hip.
- Measure along the hipline between stitching lines. Double this measurement for the actual width; record.
- Compare your hip measurement with the pattern hip measurement to determine if you need to make an adjustment.

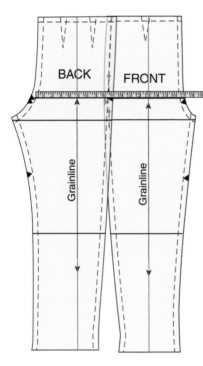

Pattern Thigh

- Pin the pant pattern pieces together at the side seams, stacking stitching lines at the crotch. (The horizontal crotchline is the same as the thigh line.)
- Measure along the crotchline between stitching lines; record.
- Compare your thigh measurement with the pattern thigh measurement to determine if you need to make an adjustment.

> ■ NOTE FROM NANCY
>
> *Remember, it's only necessary to measure the pattern's thigh width if the widest area of your figure is below the hip.*

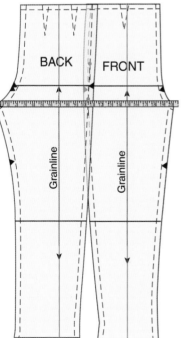

First Worksheet: Hem Length Changes

Keep fitting simple by grouping similar activities. Start by making all length adjustments on the same worksheet. Then make all width adjustments on a second worksheet. Changing the length first and the width second streamlines the process. For example, if you need to change the overall length, make this the first modification on your list. It will save both time and tracing!

Cut the worksheet longer than the pattern piece and place it under the pattern. To change the pant length, the side curve, or the crotch length, slide the pattern up or down along the grainline as you would raise or lower a window.

Hem Changes

Refer to the *Personal Fitting Chart for Pants*, page 123, to determine the amount to adjust the hem. Add or subtract the total change needed on both the front and back pattern pieces.

Lengthening

1 Outline the hem and 1" of both side seams of the front pattern piece on the first worksheet.

2 Measure up from the hemline the amount the pants need to be lengthened; mark on the worksheet.

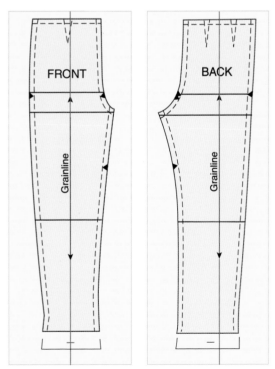

Outline hem and 1" of side seam. Measure increase above hem; mark.

3 Slide the pattern up to the mark, following the grainline. Trace the remainder of the pattern, extending the sides down to the new hemline.

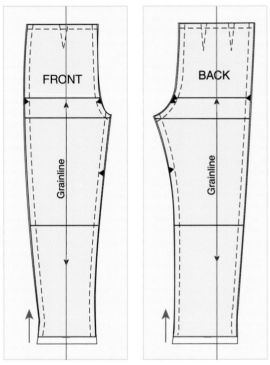

Slide pattern up; trace.

4 Match the pattern to the new outline; tape. If there are no additional length changes, cut out the pattern, following the new outline.

5 Repeat steps 1 through 4 on the back pattern piece.

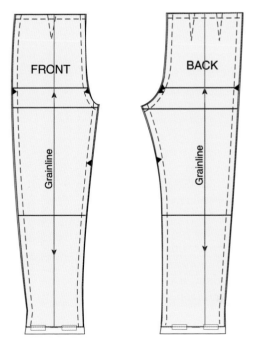

Shortening

1 Outline the hem and 1" of both side seams of the front pattern piece on the first worksheet.

2 Measure down from the hemline the amount the pants need to be shortened; mark it on the worksheet.

3 Slide the pattern down to the mark, following the grainline. Trace the remainder of the pattern, extending the sides to the new hemline.

2

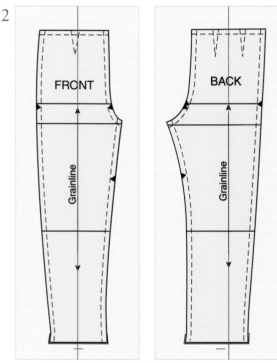

Outline hem and 1" of side seam. Measure
decrease below hem; mark.

3

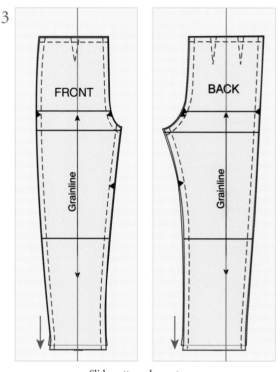

Slide pattern down; trace.

> ### ▌ NOTE FROM NANCY
>
> *If the pants are shortened a considerable amount, the new hem could appear too wide. To keep the original width, simply draw a new cuff line from the original hem width, tapering up to meet the pattern at the kneeline on both sides.*

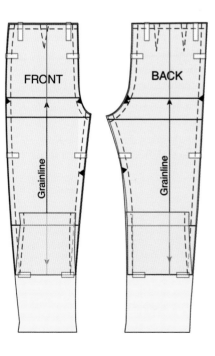

4 Match the pattern to the outline; tape. Fold in the pattern sections that overlap the new outline. If there are no additional length changes, cut out the pattern, following the new outline.

5 Repeat steps 1 through 4 on the back pattern piece.

Fitting the Side Curve

Adding length at the side adjusts for a high hip; taking away length accommodates a low, flat hip. Both fitting techniques are easily done at the side seams of the front and back pattern pieces.

Refer to the *Personal Fitting Chart for Pants*, page 123, to see if any length should be added or subtracted for a proper fit at the side curve. The total length needed will be added to or subtracted from the front and back pattern pieces.

Lengthening

1 Place the front pattern piece on the first worksheet. Use the same worksheet used to adjust the hem length. If hem length was not changed, outline the side and waist cutting lines on the worksheet. Measure up the needed increase from the waist cutting line at the side seam; mark.

2 Slide the pattern up to the mark, following the grainline. Trace the longer side cutting line.

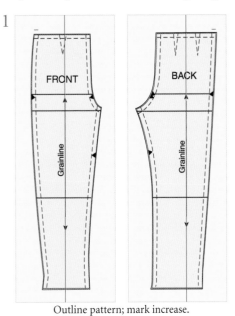

Outline pattern; mark increase.

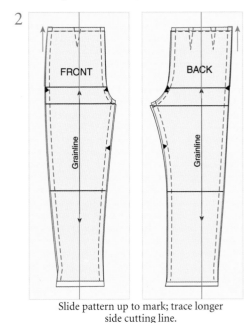

Slide pattern up to mark; trace longer side cutting line.

3 Place a pin at the point where waist and side seams intersect. Pivot the pattern down to the original waist outline. Trace new waist cutting line.

4 Match the pattern to the original outline; tape. If there are no additional length changes, cut out the pattern, following the new outline.

5 Repeat steps 1 through 4 on the back pattern piece.

> ▮ NOTE FROM NANCY
> *If one hip is higher than the other, adjust the pattern for the higher hip. It will be easy to remove length from the shorter side during the first fitting.*

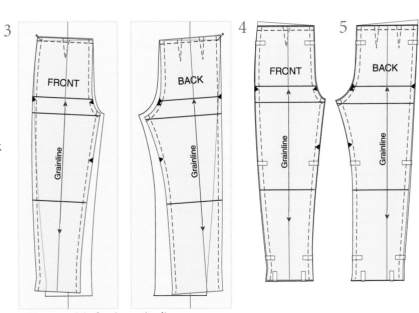

Pivot to original waist cutting line; trace.

Shortening

1. Place the front pattern piece on the first worksheet. Use the same worksheet used to adjust the hem length. If hem length was not changed, outline the side and waist cutting lines on the worksheet. Measure down the needed decrease from the waist cutting line at the side seam; mark.

2. Slide the pattern down to the mark, following the grainline.

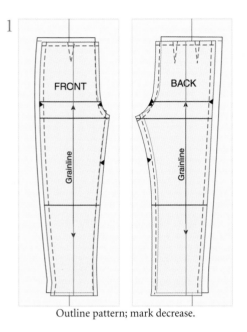

Outline pattern; mark decrease.

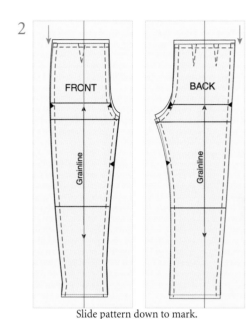

Slide pattern down to mark.

3. Place a pin at the point where the waist and side seams intersect. Pivot the pattern up to the original waist outline. Trace the new waist cutting line.

4. Match the pattern to the original outline; tape. Fold back the pattern sections that overlap the new cutting lines. If there are no additional length changes, cut out the pattern, following the new outline.

5. Repeat steps 1 through 4 on the back pattern piece.

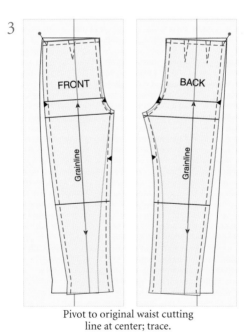

Pivot to original waist cutting line at center; trace.

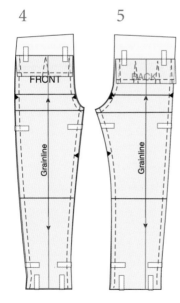

Fitting the Crotch

Crotch Adjustments

When it comes to fitting pants, most of us need a confidence booster. This section on fitting the crotch area can be the most challenging, yet we make it easier and give you the confidence you need to make the right decision by providing five options. It will not be difficult to determine which option to choose—your figure type and the adjustment amount lead you in the right direction.

Refer to the *Personal Fitting Chart for Pants*, page 123, for the amount to be added to or subtracted from the crotch area. Divide the needed adjustment by two, since the amount will be added or subtracted evenly to the front and the back.

▌NOTE FROM NANCY

Pant patterns are drafted the way most of us are shaped—
with a slight curve in the front and a fuller curve in the back.
To give us sitting room, the back pattern is 2" to 3" longer
than the front.

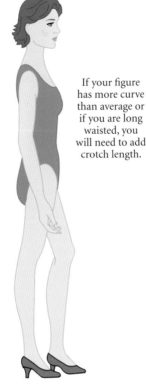

If your figure has more curve than average or if you are long waisted, you will need to add crotch length.

Lengthening 4" or Less

1　Place the front pattern piece on the first worksheet. If this is the first adjustment you are making, outline the pattern cutting lines on the worksheet. Measure down from the crotch cutting line the needed increase amount; mark.

2　Slide the pattern down to the mark, following the grainline.

3　Trace the lower part of the new crotchline and the changed portion of the inseam on the worksheet.

4　Match the pattern to the original outline; tape. Fold back the pattern sections that overlap the new cutting lines. If there are no additional length changes, cut out the pattern, following the new outline.

5　Repeat steps 1 through 4 on the back pattern piece.

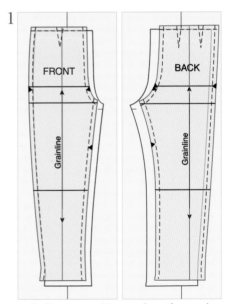

Outline pattern. Measure down from each crotch cutting line; mark increase.

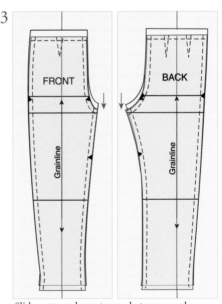

Slide pattern down to mark, trace new longer crotchline and changes to inseam.

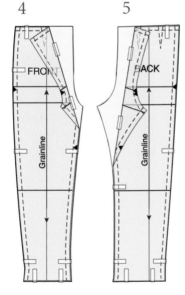

Shortening 4" or Less

1 Place the front pattern piece on the first worksheet. If this is the first adjustment you are making, outline the pattern cutting lines on the worksheet. Measure up from the crotch cutting line the needed decrease amount; mark.

2 Slide the pattern up to the mark, following the grainline.

3 Trace the raised part of the new crotchline and the changed portion of the inseam on the worksheet.

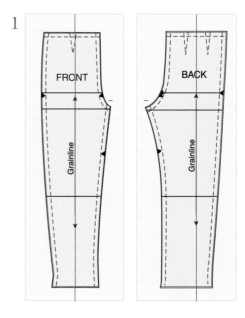

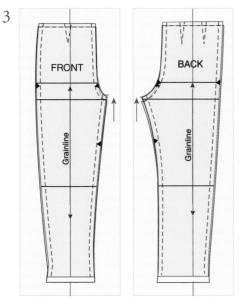

Slide pattern up to mark; trace new raised crotchline and changes to inseam.

4 Match the pattern to the original outline; tape. If there are no additional length changes, cut out the pattern, following the new outline.

5 Repeat steps 1 through 4 on the back pattern piece.

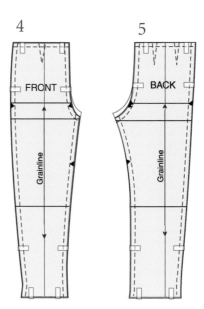

Fitting the Crotch, continued

Lengthening 4" or More

If the crotch needs to be lengthened 4" or more, make part of the adjustment at the crotch points and part at the center front or the center back. There are three possibilities; choose the option that best fits your shape.

Option 1: Full Figure

A full figure has a rounded tummy and a predominant seat curve. Refer to the *Personal Fitting Chart for Pants*, page 123, for the amount to add to the crotch area.

- Add 1" above the waist cutting lines at the center front and back.
- Divide the remaining increase between both the front and back crotch points. For example, if you need to add 6", add 1" above the original outline at the center front and 1" above the center back. Then lower both the front and back crotch points 2" each.

1 Place the front pattern piece on the first worksheet. If this is the first adjustment for this pattern, outline the cutting lines. Measure and mark the points determined above.

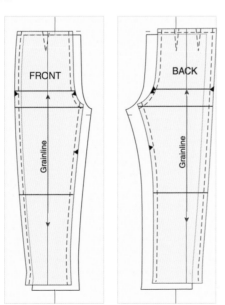

Outline. Measure and mark increases at waist and crotch points on center front and center back pieces.

2 Slide the pattern to change the crotchline.
- Lengthen the crotch by sliding the front pattern piece down to the crotch mark, following the grainline. Trace the lower part of the new crotchline and the changed portion of the inseam.

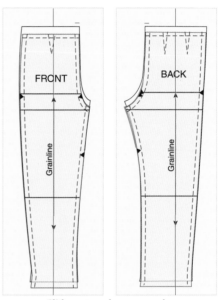

Slide pattern down to mark.

- Add waist length by sliding the pattern up to the new center front mark, following the grainline. Trace the longer crotchline. Do not move the pattern.

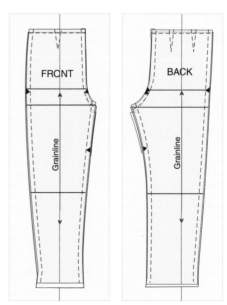

Slide pattern up to waist increase; trace longer crotchline.

3 Place a pin at the point where waist and crotch seams intersect. Pivot the pattern out to the original side cutting line. Trace the new waist cutting line.

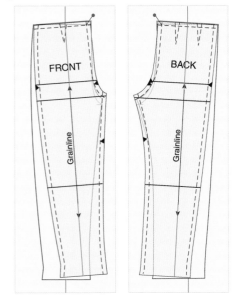

Pivot to original side cutting line; trace new waist cutting line.

4 Match the pattern to the original outline; tape. Fold back the pattern sections that overlap the new outline. If there are no additional length changes, cut out the pattern, following the new outline.

5 Repeat steps 1 through 4 on the back pattern piece.

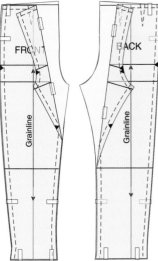

Option 2: Predominant Tummy

This figure type has a large curve in the tummy area and less of a curve in the seat. Refer to the *Personal Fitting Chart for Pants*, page 123, for the amount to add to the crotch area.

- Add 1" above the waist cutting line at the center front only.
- Divide the remaining increase between both the front and back crotch points. For example, if you need to add 5", add 1" above the outline at the center front. Then lower both the front and back crotch points 2" each.

1 Place the front and back pattern pieces on the first worksheets. If this is the first modification for this pattern, outline the cutting lines. Measure and mark the points determined above.

2 Slide the front pattern piece down to the crotch mark, following the grainline. Trace the lower part of the crotchline and the changed portion of the inseam. Repeat on the back pattern piece.

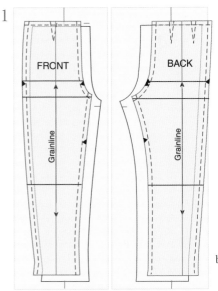

Outline. Measure and mark increases at front waist and both crotch points.

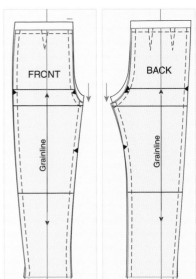

Slide pattern down to mark; trace.

Fitting the Crotch, *continued*

3 Slide the front pattern piece up along the grainline to the center front mark. Trace the longer crotchline. Do not move the pattern.

4 Place a pin at the point where the waist and crotch seams intersect. Pivot the front pattern piece in to the original side cutting line. Trace the new waist cutting line.

5 Match the pattern pieces to the original outline and tape. Fold back the pattern sections that overlap the new outline. If there are no additional length changes, cut out the pattern, following the new outline.

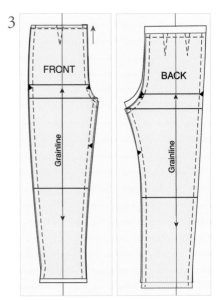
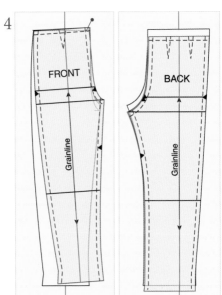
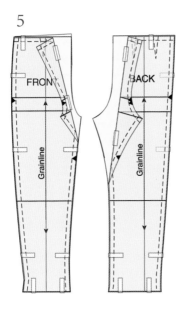

Slide front pattern piece up to center front mark; trace longer crotchline.

Pivot to original side cutting line, trace new waist cutting line.

Option 3: Predominant Seat

This figure type has a greater curve in the seat area. Refer to the *Personal Fitting Chart for Pants*, page 123, for the amount to add to the crotch area.

- Add 1" above the waist cutting line at the center back only.
- Divide the remaining increase between both the front and back crotch points. For example, if you need to add 7", add 1" above the outline at the center back. Then lower both the front and back crotch points 3" each.

1 Place the front and back pattern pieces on the first worksheets. If this is the first adjustment for this pattern, outline the cutting lines. Measure and mark the points determined above.

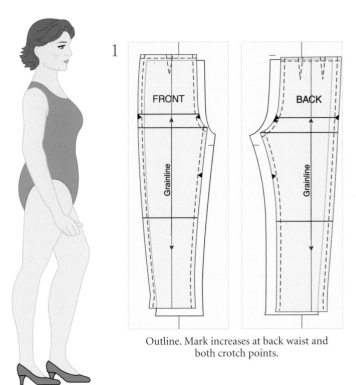

Outline. Mark increases at back waist and both crotch points.

2   Slide the front and back pattern pieces down to the new crotch marks, following the grainline. Trace the lower part of the crotchline and the changed portion of the inseam.

3   Add waist length to the back pattern piece by sliding the pattern up along the grainline to the center back mark. Trace the longer crotchline. Do not move the pattern.

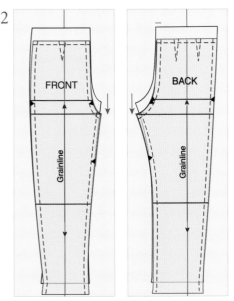 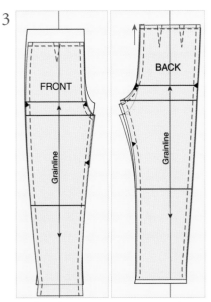

Slide down to crotch mark; trace.

Slide back pattern piece to waist mark;
trace longer back crotchline.

4   Place a pin on the back pattern at the point where the waist and crotch intersect. Pivot the back pattern piece in to the original side cutting line. Trace the new waist cutting line.

5   Match both pattern pieces to the original outlines; tape. Fold back the pattern sections that overlap the new outline. If there are no additional length changes, cut out the pattern, following the new outline.

 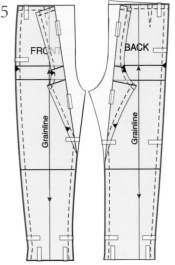

Pivot back to original side cutting line;
trace new waist cutting line.

Cut out pattern following new outline.

Second Worksheet: Waist Width Changes

To make the three width fitting changes simply pivot the pattern. Anchor the pattern with a pin and move it like the pendulum of a clock to add or subtract inches.

All length changes were completed on one worksheet, and all width changes can be completed on a second worksheet. Cut out the first worksheet with the length changes, following the new cutting lines. Match the pattern to the original outline and tape the pattern to the worksheet. Fold in any pattern sections that overlap the new outline.

The combination of the original pattern and the first worksheet becomes your new pattern. Use this new pattern as your guideline for outlining width changes.

For ease in pivoting for width changes, separate directions explain how to change the waist, hip, and thigh. The end of the chapter shows how to combine several common modifications. If you need two or more width changes, read through the individual sections and then refer to the end of the chapter for the appropriate combination.

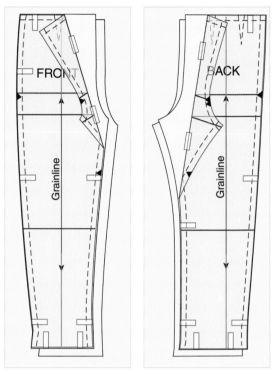

First worksheet becomes pattern for making width changes.

Fitting the Waist

Refer to the *Personal Fitting Chart for Pants*, page 123, for the amount to modify the waist. Divide the waist adjustment amount by eight (the number of cut edges on the four seams).

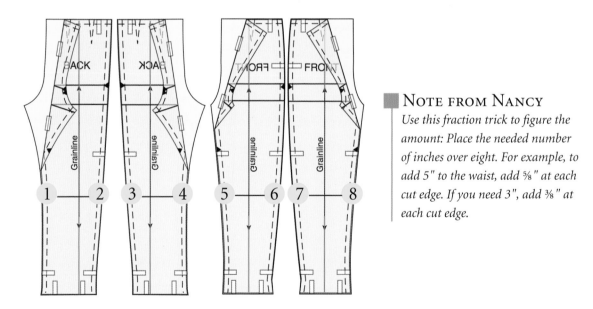

Note from Nancy

Use this fraction trick to figure the amount: Place the needed number of inches over eight. For example, to add 5" to the waist, add ⅝" at each cut edge. If you need 3", add ⅜" at each cut edge.

To increase the waist, add the divided increase to the waist on both the front and back pattern pieces. To decrease the waist, subtract the divided decrease from the waist on both the front and back pattern pieces.

Increasing

1 Place the front pattern piece on the second worksheet. Outline the cutting lines. Measure the needed increase out on both sides of the waist cutting line; mark.

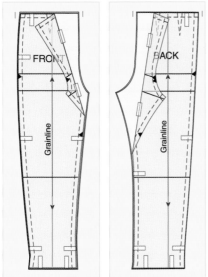

Outline pattern. Measure increase; mark on both sides.

▌NOTE FROM NANCY

As a reminder, if you made length changes, use the first worksheet as the pattern. If you didn't make any length changes, use the original pattern.

2 Increase at the side seam.
- Place a pin at the hipline stitching line. Pivot the pattern out to the increase mark. Trace the new cutting line between the waist and the hip.
- Extend the waist cutting line to the new width.
- Match the pattern to the original outline.

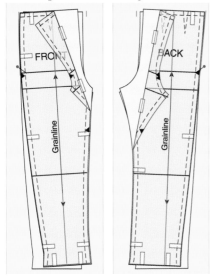

Pivot to increase on side seam; trace new cutting line between waist and hip.

3 Increase the waist at the center seam.
- Place a pin at the hipline stitching line. Pivot the pattern out to the increase mark. Trace the new cutting line between the waist and the hip.
- Extend the waist cutting line to the new width.

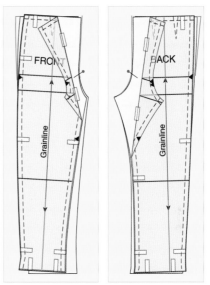

Pivot to increase at center seam; trace new center cutting line.

4 Match the pattern to the original outline; tape. If there are no additional width changes, cut out the pattern, following the new outline.

5 Repeat steps 1 through 4 on the back pattern piece.

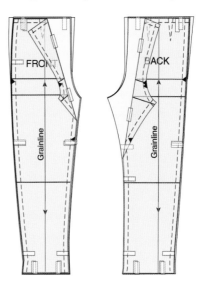

▌NOTE FROM NANCY

See *Adjusting the Waistband on pages 62–63.*

Decreasing

1 Place the front pattern piece on the second worksheet. Outline the cutting lines. Measure in from both sides of the waist cutting line; mark.

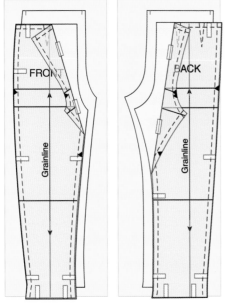

Outline pattern. Measure in needed decrease from both sides of waist cutting line; mark.

2 Decrease at the side seam.
- Place a pin at the hipline stitching line. Pivot the pattern in to the decrease mark. Trace the new cutting line between the waist and the hip.
- Match the pattern piece to the original outline.

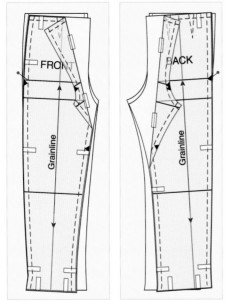

Pivot to decrease mark at side seam; trace new cutting line between waist and hip.

3 Decrease at the center seam.
- Place a pin at the hipline stitching line. Pivot the pattern in to the decrease mark.
- Trace the new cutting line between the waist and the hip.

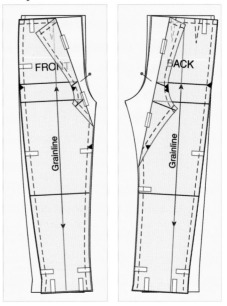

Pivot to increase mark at center seam; trace new center cutting line.

4 Match the pattern to the original outline; tape. Fold back the pattern sections that overlap the new outline. If there are no other width changes, cut out the pattern, following the new outline.

5 Repeat steps 1 through 4 on the back pattern piece.

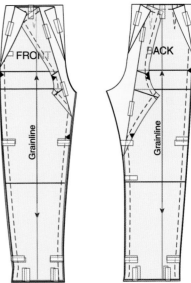

■ **NOTE FROM NANCY**
See Adjusting the Waistband *on pages 62–63.*

Fitting the Hip

If you purchased a pattern smaller than your hip measurement (using the chart on page 123), you will need to increase the hip of your pattern. The change is easy, and the fit you'll achieve will be worth the time spent making this simple adjustment.

Increasing

Refer to the *Personal Fitting Chart for Pants*, page 123, to determine the amount to change the hip. Divide that number by eight (the number of cut edges on the four seams).

1 Place the front pattern piece on the second worksheet. If this is the first width change for this pattern, outline the pattern. Measure the needed increase out on both sides of the hip cutting lines; mark.

2 Increase at the side seam.
 • Place a pin at the kneeline stitching line. Pivot the pattern out to the increase mark. Trace the new cutting line between the knee and the hip. Do not move the pattern.
 • Move the pin to the hipline stitching line. Pivot the pattern to the original waist outline. Trace the new cutting line between the hip and the waist. Match the pattern piece to the original outline.

3 Increase at the inseam and the center seam.
 • Place a pin at the kneeline stitching line. Pivot the pattern out to the increase mark. Trace the new cutting line between the knee and the hip. Keep the pattern pivoted.

1

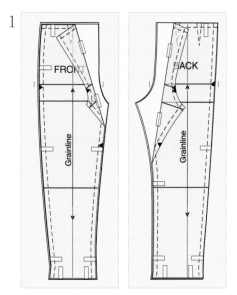

Outline pattern. Measure increase on both sides of hip cutting lines; mark.

2

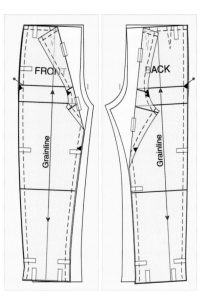

Pivot to increase on side cutting line; trace.

Pivot to waist; trace new cutting line between hip and waist.

3

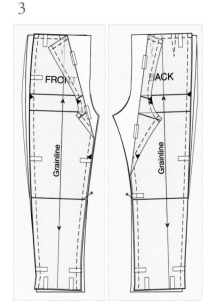

Pivot to increase at inseam; trace new cutting line between knee and hip.

Fitting the Hip, continued

- Move the pin to the hipline stitching line; pivot the pattern to the original outline at the waist. Trace the new cutting line between the hip and the waist.

4 Match the pattern to the original outline; tape. If there are no other width changes, cut out the pattern, following the new outline.

5 Repeat steps 1 through 4 on the back pattern piece.

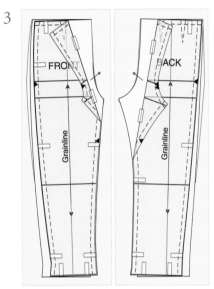

Pivot to waist; trace between hip and waist.

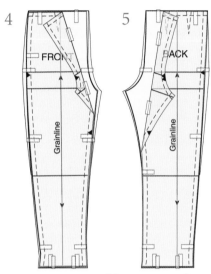

Cut out pattern following new outline.

Fitting the Thigh

Using the chart on page 123, you purchased a pattern smaller than your hip to give a better fit in the thigh and the crotch. For that reason, you should not need to decrease the thigh. Remember, it's easier to make a pattern larger than smaller.

Increasing

Refer to the *Personal Fitting Chart for Pants*, page 123, to determine the amount to add to the thigh. Divide the increase by four (the number of seam edges in each pant leg).

1 Place the front pattern piece on the second worksheet. If this is the first width adjustment, outline the pattern. Measure the needed increase at the cutting line on each end of the crotchline; mark.

2 Increase at the side seam.
- Place a pin at the kneeline stitching line. Pivot the pattern out to the increase mark. Trace the new cutting line between the knee and the crotch mark. Keep the pattern pivoted.

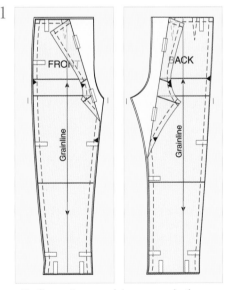

Outline pattern; mark increase on both ends of crotchline.

- Move the pin to the crotchline stitching line; pivot the pattern to the waist outline. Trace the new cutting line between the crotch and the waist. Match the pattern piece to the original outline.

2

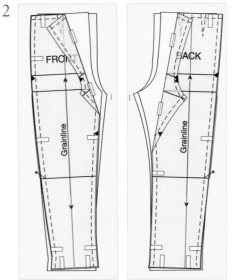

Pivot to increase mark at crotchline; trace new cutting line between knee and crotch.

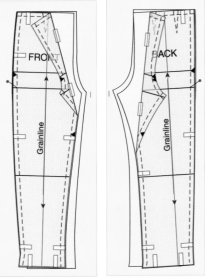

Pivot to waist; trace new cutting line between crotch and waist.

3 Increase at the inseam and the center seam.
- Place the pin at the kneeline stitching line. Pivot the pattern piece to the increase mark. Trace the new cutting line between the knee and the crotch. Keep the pattern pivoted.
- Move the pin to the crotchline stitching line. Pivot the pattern to the waist outline. Trace the new cutting line between the crotch and the waist.

4 Match pattern to original outline; tape. If there are no other width changes, cut out pattern, following the new outline.

5 Repeat steps 1 through 4 on the back pattern piece.

3

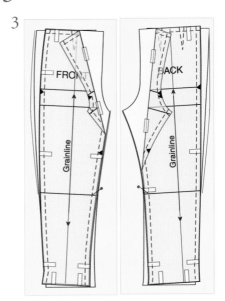

Pivot to increase mark on the inseam; trace new cutting line between knee and crotch.

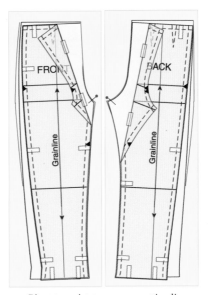

Pivot to waist; trace new cutting line between crotch and waist.

4   5

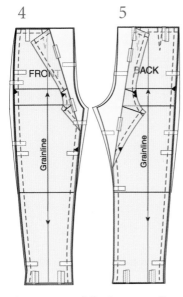

Cut out pattern following new outline.

Width Combinations

Increased Waist and Hip

As you gain fitting confidence you can easily combine pattern changes. One of the most common combinations involves increasing both the waist and the hip.

Refer to the *Personal Fitting Chart for Pants*, page 123, for the amounts to increase the waist and the hip. Divide the increase by eight.

1 Place the front pattern piece on the second worksheet; outline the pattern. Measure the needed increases out on both sides of the hip and both sides of the waist cutting lines; mark.

2 Increase at the side seam.

 • Place a pin at the kneeline stitching line. Pivot the pattern out to the hip increase mark. Trace the new cutting line between the knee and the hip. Keep the pattern pivoted.

 • Move the pin to the hipline stitching line. Pivot the pattern to the waist increase mark. Trace the new cutting line between the hip and the waist.

 • Extend the waist cutting line to the new width.

 • Match the pattern to the original outline.

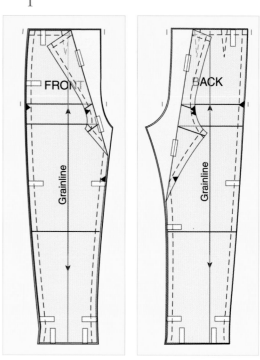

1

Outline pattern. Measure needed increase on both sides of hip and both sides of waist; mark.

2

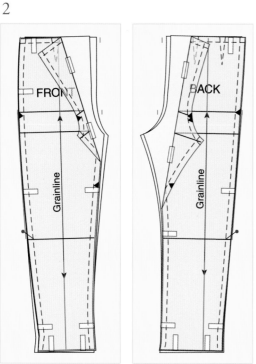 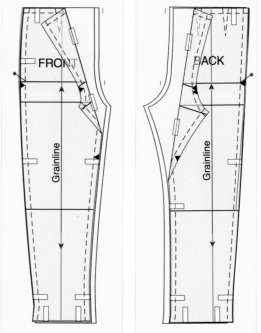

Pivot to hip increase at side seam; trace new cutting line between knee and hip.

Pivot to waist increase at side seam; trace new cutting line between hip and waist. Extend waist cutting line.

3 Adjust the inseam and the center seam.

- Place a pin at the kneeline stitching line; pivot the pattern out to the hip increase mark. Trace the new cutting line between the knee and the hip. Keep the pattern pivoted.

- Move the pin to the hipline stitching line; pivot the pattern to the waist increase mark. Trace the new cutting line between the hip and the waist.

- Extend the waist cutting line to meet the new width.

3

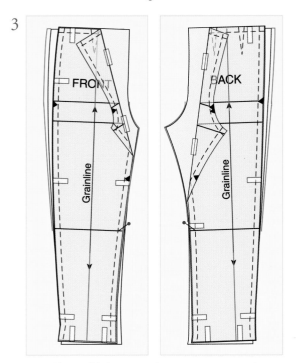

Pivot to hip increase at inseam; trace new cutting line from knee to hip.

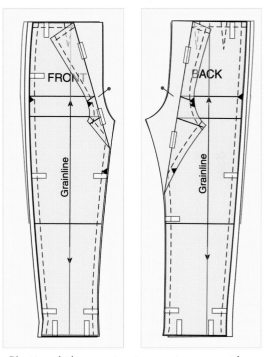

Pivot to waist increase at center seam; trace new cutting line from hip to waist. Extend waist cutting line.

4 Match the pattern to the original outline; tape. Cut out the pattern, following the new outline.

5 Repeat steps 1 through 4 on the back pattern piece.

NOTE FROM NANCY

If you need to increase the hip and decrease the waist, simply pivot in to the waist decrease mark. It's that simple!

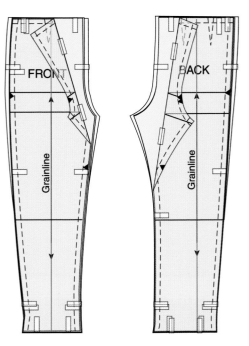

Increased Waist, Hip and Thigh Combination

When you use the *Pant Pattern Size Chart*, page 123, to choose your pattern size, you may need to increase at the waist, the hip, and the thigh. This is certain to be the case if your hip measurement is greater than 50" since I recommend against buying patterns larger than Misses' size 22. Don't worry, though, because pivot and slide techniques make this triple combination easy.

Refer to the *Personal Fitting Chart for Pants*, page 123, for the amounts to increase. Divide the needed increase for the thigh by four (four cut edges per two seams in each pant leg); divide the needed increases for the waist and the hip by eight.

1 Place the front pattern piece on the second worksheet; outline the pattern. Measure and mark the needed increases on both sides of the crotch (for the thigh), hip, and waist cutting lines.

2 Increase at the side seam.
- Place a pin at the kneeline stitching line. Pivot the pattern out to the increase mark at the crotchline. Trace the new cutting line between the knee and the crotch. Keep the pattern pivoted.

- Move the pin to the crotchline stitching line. Pivot the pattern to the increase mark at the hip. Trace the new cutting line between the crotch and the hip. Keep the pattern pivoted.

- Move the pin to the hipline stitching line. Pivot the pattern to the increase mark at the waist. Trace the new cutting line between the hip and the waist.

- Move the pattern back to the original outline.

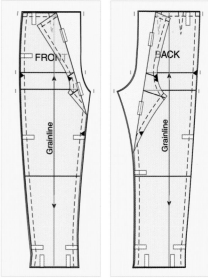

Outline pattern. Measure needed increases on both sides of crotch (thigh), hip, and waist cutting lines; mark.

2

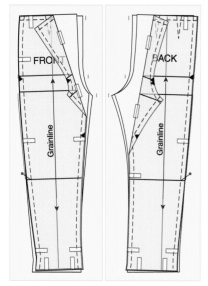

Pivot to increase at crotch line; trace new cutting line between knee and crotch.

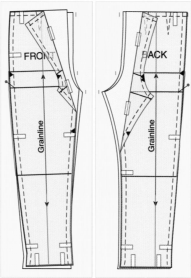

Pivot to increase at side seam; trace new cutting line between waist and hip.

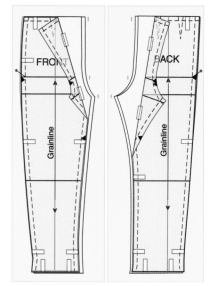

Pivot to waist increase at side seam; trace new cutting line between hip and waist.

3 Adjust at the inseam and the center seam.
- Place a pin at the kneeline stitching line; pivot the pattern out to the increase mark at the crotchline. Trace the new cutting line between the knee and the crotch mark. Keep the pattern piece pivoted.

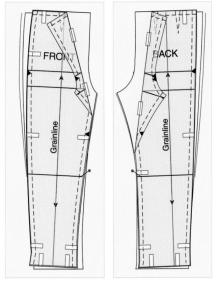

Pivot to crotch increase at inseam; trace new cutting line between knee and crotch.

- Move the pin to the crotchline stitching line; pivot the pattern to the increase mark at the hip. Trace the new cutting line between the crotch and the hip. Keep the pattern pivoted.

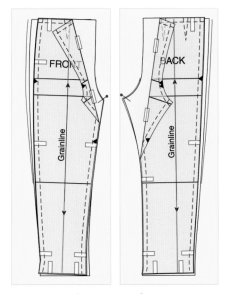

Pivot to crotch increase mark at center seam; trace new cutting line between crotch and hip.

- Move the pin to the hipline stitching line; pivot the pattern to the increase mark at the waist. Trace the new cutting line between the hip and the waist.

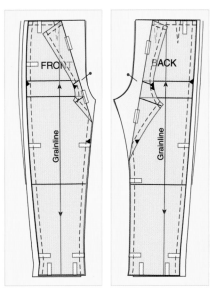

Pivot to waist increase mark at center seam; trace new cutting line between hip and waist.

4 Match the pattern to the original outline; tape. Cut out the pattern, following the new outline.

5 Repeat steps 1 through 4 on the back pattern piece.

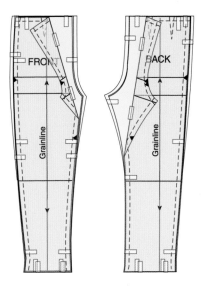

CHAPTER SIX

Fine-Tuning the Fit

Minor pattern changes will improve not only the way your clothes look on you, but also the way you feel in them. Fine-tune your fit and find finesse!

Checking the Fit

Throughout this book, I've asked you to use a classic-style pattern for your first pivot and slide adjustment. That's because this simple styling makes it easy to check the fit.

Machine Basting Fabric Pieces

After cutting out the pattern, machine baste the basic pieces together. Use a machine basting stitch and slightly loosen the top tension to make removing the stitches an easy process. Use the order given below.

For Blouses, Dresses and Jackets:
- Darts
- Shoulder seams
- Center front or center back and side seams
- Sleeve underarm seam
- Armhole seam for set-in sleeves

For Skirts:
- Pleats, darts, or gathers
- Center front, center back, and side seams (Do not close zipper opening.)

For Pants:
- Pleats, darts, or gathers
- Inseams
- Center front and center back crotch (Do not close zipper opening.)
- Side seams

Machine-basted blouse

Machine-basted dress

Machine-basted pants

Machine-basted jacket

Machine-basted skirt

Trying on the Garment

> **NOTE FROM NANCY**
>
> *Have your sewing buddy help you fine-tune the fit. If you have to work alone, do the best you can. Remember, any improvement will make your garment fit better than most ready-to-wear clothes.*

For Blouses, Tops, Jackets and Dresses:

- Pin the shoulder pads in place, if required.
- Try on the garment, pinning closed the center front or center back opening.

For Skirts and Pants:

- Use a safety pin, and pin a length of 1" wide elastic together to fit your waist.
- Pin the skirt or the pants to the elastic, matching the ⅝" waist stitching line to the center of the elastic.

Pin in shoulder pads; pin garment closed at center front.

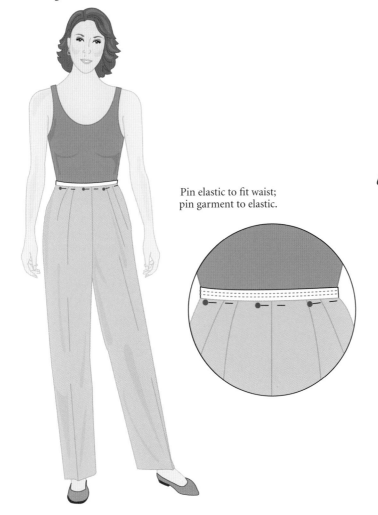

Pin elastic to fit waist;
pin garment to elastic.

Checking for Wrinkles

If your garment has fitting problems, they will show up as wrinkles when you try it on. Before analyzing the fit of your garment, it is important to understand the different types of wrinkles.

Most sewing books group wrinkles into just three categories: horizontal, vertical, and bias. However, before you look at their direction, it is more useful to determine whether the wrinkles are actually folds of excess fabric or pulls caused by too little fabric. This means that there are actually six types of wrinkles, not three.

After identifying the wrinkles, adjust the garment and the pattern pieces, using the instructions detailed in this chapter. To help you understand how to make these fine-tuning changes, refer to the following examples from each of the six wrinkle categories.

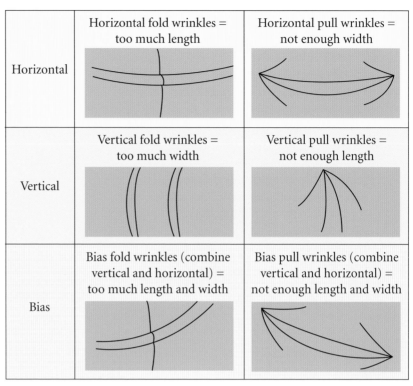

Horizontal	Horizontal fold wrinkles = too much length	Horizontal pull wrinkles = not enough width
Vertical	Vertical fold wrinkles = too much width	Vertical pull wrinkles = not enough length
Bias	Bias fold wrinkles (combine vertical and horizontal) = too much length and width	Bias pull wrinkles (combine vertical and horizontal) = not enough length and width

Horizontal Fold Wrinkles

A horizontal fold wrinkle occurs when there is too much length in a pattern. A common horizontal fold wrinkle occurs on skirts or pants directly below the back waist, indicating a swayback.

1 Measure the extra fold of the fabric and record the amount.

- Pinch and pin the extra fold of fabric below the waist.

- Measure the depth of the wrinkle at the deepest part; double this measurement to determine the total wrinkle amount.

- Record the wrinkle amount on your *Personal Fitting Chart for Pants*, page 123, in the special measurements column.

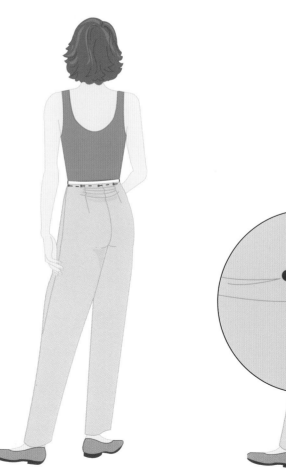

2 Take off the garment; remove the basting stitches and the pins.

3 Make fitting changes on the fabric pieces.
- Fold the pant back in half with right sides together. Measure the wrinkle amount down from the cutting edge at the center back (see step 1). Place a pin in the fabric at this point.
- Place the pant back pattern piece on top of the actual pant back; slide the pattern down until the cutting line meets the pin.

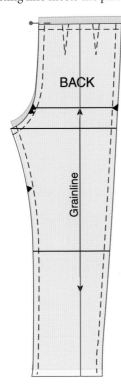

- At the center back of the pattern, insert a pin at the point where the waist and crotch seamlines intersect. Pivot the pattern to the waist cutting line at the side seam.

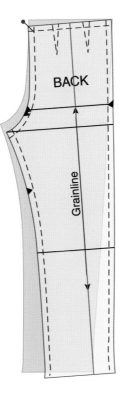

- Trim the excess fabric, following the pattern cutting line. Save this fabric.

4 Use the fabric as a template to make the same adjustment on the pattern piece.

5 Make fitting changes for a swayback on all future sewing project patterns.

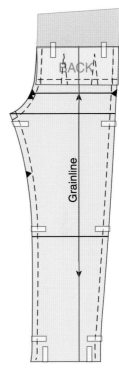

NOTE FROM NANCY

If you notice this horizontal fold wrinkle after the waistband has been attached (or in a ready-to-wear garment), you can still correct it. Clip the back waist stitches between the side seams and make the fitting changes. If the garment has a back zipper, open the zipper so the zipper pull is below the new cut edge. Then bartack on each side just below the new cut edge and trim the excess zipper.

Checking for Wrinkles, continued

Horizontal Pull Wrinkles

Horizontal wrinkles that pull show that a garment is too tight. It is common to find these wrinkles at the bust, the waist, or the hip.

1. Clip the side seam basting stitches between the waist and the hem.

2. Restitch the seam by machine basting a ¼" to ⅜" seam allowance. This will add 1" to 1½".

3. Try on the pants. If you still have wrinkles, sew a shallower seam using 15 stitches per inch. Zigzag or serge the edges together; press the seam allowance to one side.

4. Measure; record the hip changes on the *Personal Fitting Chart for Pants*, page 123.

5. Mark the new stitching line on the pattern pieces. For future sewing projects, increase the hip for skirts as detailed on page 64 or for pants as shown on page 94.

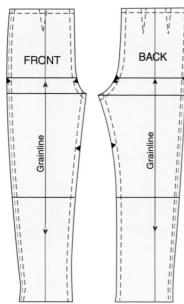

FRONT   BACK

Grainline   Grainline

■ NOTE FROM NANCY

When adding room to the hip of a skirt, be sure to add the same increase all the way to the hem. If you take a narrower seam allowance just at the hip, the grainline will be distorted, causing the skirt to curve in at the bottom, which emphasizes the hip.

Vertical Fold Wrinkles

Vertical fold wrinkles indicate that the pattern is too wide. A common example of a vertical fold wrinkle occurs across the back shoulder.

1. Measure the fold and record the amount.
   - Pinch and pin the extra fold of fabric on each side of the back.

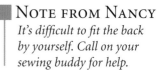

■ NOTE FROM NANCY

It's difficult to fit the back by yourself. Call on your sewing buddy for help.

- Measure the deepest part of the wrinkle; double this measurement to determine the total wrinkle amount. You will remove that amount from each side of the armhole area.
- Record the measurement on the *Personal Fitting Chart*, page 122.

2 Take off the garment; remove the basting stitches and the pins.

3 Make fitting changes on the fabric pieces.

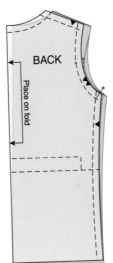

- Fold the back fabric pieces with right sides together. At the center of the armhole on the garment, measure the wrinkle amount in from the cut edge (see step 1). Mark with a pin.
- Measure the same distance in from the cut edge at the underarm. Mark with a pin.
- Place the back pattern piece on top of the fabric; mark a pivot point at the center of the armhole.
- Place a pin at the intersection of the shoulder and armhole. Pivot the pattern in to the marking pin at the center of the armhole.
- Remove the pin. With a fabric marking pen, trace the new cutting line on the fabric between the shoulder and the center of the armhole.

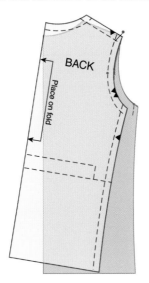

- Keeping the pattern pivoted, move the pin to pivot point at the center of the armhole. Pivot the pattern out to the marking pin at the underarm. Trace the remainder of the armhole cutting line on the fabric between the center of the armhole and the underarm. Remove the pin.
- Insert a pin at intersection of the armhole and side seam. Pivot the pattern out to the cut edge of the fabric at the waist. Trace the new cutting line on the fabric from the underarm to the waist.

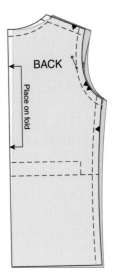

4 Trim the excess fabric following the pattern cutting line. Use the fabric piece(s) as a template to make the same adjustment on the pattern piece.

5 Make fitting changes for a narrow back on all future projects.

Vertical Pull Wrinkles

Common vertical pull wrinkles occur along the center back, indicating that the back length is too short.

1 Clip the waist stitches.

2 Sew a narrower seam allowance at the waist, tapering to a normal seam allowance at the side seams.

3 Measure and record changes on the *Personal Fitting Chart* on page 122.

4 Mark the needed change on the pattern piece.

5 For future sewing projects, make fitting changes on the pattern piece for a longer back length as detailed in *Curved Back*, page 40.

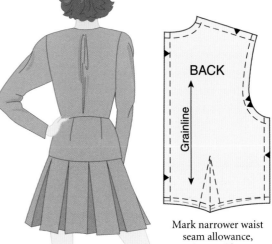

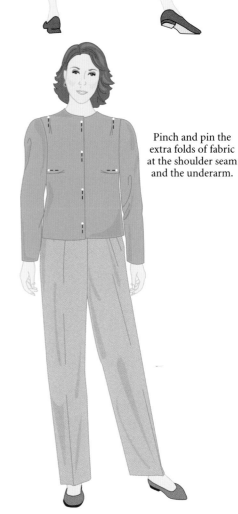

Mark narrower waist seam allowance, tapering to side seam.

Bias Fold Wrinkles

Bias fold wrinkles indicate too much length and width. One example is when the shoulder seam is too wide and the underarm seam is too long. Have your sewing buddy help you pinch and pin the wrinkles in this area.

1 Measure the extra folds of fabric and record.

- Pinch and pin the extra folds of fabric at the shoulder seam (vertical) and the underarm (horizontal) on the garment front.
- Measure the depth of one vertical fold wrinkle; double the measurement for the total vertical wrinkle amount per side.
- Measure the depth of one horizontal fold wrinkle; double the measurement to determine the total horizontal wrinkle amount per side.
- Record both amounts (vertical and horizontal) on the *Personal Fitting Chart*, page 122.
- Repeat step 1 to measure wrinkle folds for the garment back.

Pinch and pin the extra folds of fabric at the shoulder seam and the underarm.

2 Take off the garment; remove the basting stitches and the pins.

3 Make fitting changes on the fabric.
   - Fold the fabric front in half with right sides together.
   - Measure the vertical wrinkle amount in from the end of the shoulder cutting line. Place a pin vertically in the fabric at this point.
   - Measure the horizontal wrinkle amount down from the cutting line at the end of the shoulder. Place a pin horizontally in the fabric at this point.
   - Place the front pattern piece on top of the fabric. Slide the pattern along the shoulder cutting line until the cutting line at the end of the shoulder meets the vertical pin.
   - Place a pin at the intersection of the shoulder and neckline seams. Pivot the pattern to the horizontal pin at the end of the shoulder. Using a fabric marking pen, trace the new shoulder cutting line.

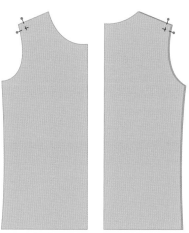

Mark changes with pins at shoulder and armhole.

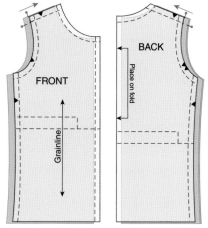

Slide along shoulder seam to vertical marking.

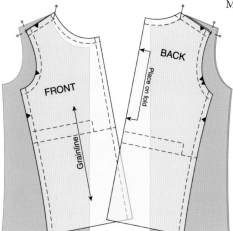

Pivot; trace new shoulder cutting line.

NOTE FROM NANCY
If you're shortening more than ⅝" your pivot pin will be off the fabric. Simply move the pivot pin in (perpendicular to the grainline) until you reach the fabric stitching line and pivot from this point.

   - Keeping the pattern pivoted, place a pin at the intersection of the shoulder and armhole seams. Pivot the pattern to the actual cut fabric at the underarm. Trace the new armhole cutting line with a fabric marking pen.

4 Trim the excess fabric, following the pattern cutting line. Use the fabric piece as a template to make the same adjustment on the pattern piece.

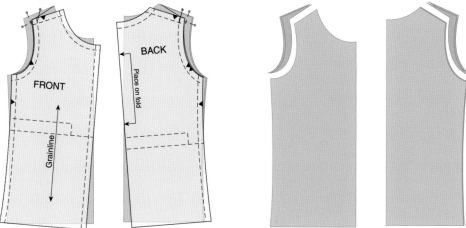

5 For future sewing projects, make fitting changes on the pattern for narrow shoulders, pages 32–33, and for sloping shoulders, pages 32 and 36.

Checking for Wrinkles, continued

Bias Pull Wrinkles

A common bias pull wrinkle occurs below the waist, indicating that one hip is higher than the other.

1 Ask your sewing buddy to help you unpin the skirt from the elastic around your waist. Clip the side seam stitches until you have eliminated the wrinkles.

2 Sew a narrower side seam. Mark a narrower waist seam on the front and the back of the higher hip side—the side with the wrinkles.

3 Measure and record the changes on the *Personal Fitting Chart* on page 122.

4 Mark the new stitching lines on the front and back pattern pieces, noting the side with the higher hip.

5 For future sewing projects, make fitting changes on the pattern for a high hip as described on pages 66 and 84.

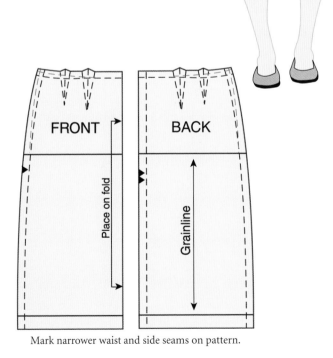

Bias pull wrinkles

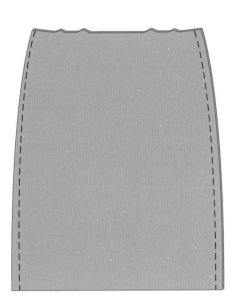

Sew narrower side seam on higher hip side.

Mark narrower waist and side seams on pattern.

Fine-Tuning Pants Fitting

The examples used to detail the six common wrinkles apply to fitting pants, yet fine-tuning the fit in pants is generally more of a challenge than fitting other garments.

Pant wrinkles, especially in the crotch area, aren't always evident until the pants are sewn. Here are a few more wrinkle-solving alternatives to use during the fine-tuning stage, or even after the pants are completed.

Crotch Wrinkles

Horizontal folds under the seat are probably the most common wrinkle in pants. This wrinkle indicates that the inseam length is too long and the crotch length is too short. The following steps will help you easily remove these wrinkles.

1   Turn the pants wrong side out; stitch a deeper crotch seam. Sew a ½" deeper seam where the crotch curves, both on the front and the back; trim the excess seam allowance.

2   Try on your pants. If you still see a wrinkle, repeat step 1 with a ¼" deeper seam allowance.

3   Record the change on the *Personal Fitting Chart for Pants*, page 123.

4   Mark the changes on the pattern pieces.

5   On future projects, lengthen the crotch as detailed beginning on page 86.

Horizontal fold wrinkles under seat

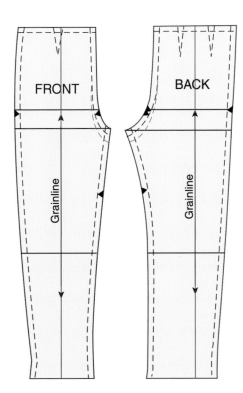

Mark a deeper seam in crotch curve.

FRONT   BACK

Grainline   Grainline

Fine-Tuning Pants Fitting, continued

Correcting Uneven Front Creases

Hanging Inward

If the side length is too long, the center front creases will bow in.

1 Unpin the pants from the elastic at the side seam, smooth the fabric up until the center front crease hangs straight; repin the pants to the elastic.

Repin pants to elastic until creases hang straight.

2 Take off the pants.

3 Mark the new waist stitching line and a ⅝" seam above the stitching line on the pant front and back.

4 Make fitting changes on the pants.
 • Fold the pants, right sides together, at the center front; place the front pattern piece on the fabric.
 • Match the pattern and the fabric at the original center front line.
 • Place a pin at the intersection of waistline and crotch. Pivot pattern down to the new cutting line marked on the pant side seam.
 • Trim the excess fabric at the waist along the pattern cutting line.
 • Repeat steps 3 and 4 on the back pattern piece.

5 Use the fabric as a template to make the same adjustment on the front and back pattern pieces.

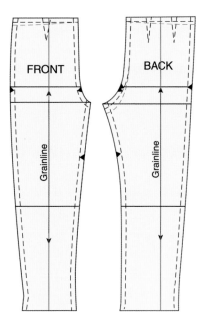

6 Record the changes on the *Personal Fitting Chart for Pants*, page 123.

On future projects, shorten the side curve on the pattern as detailed on page 75.

■ NOTE FROM NANCY
If only one crease bows in, trim only that side of your pants, both front and back.

Hanging Outward

If one hip is higher than the other by even a slight amount, it may now become noticeable with the crease of one pant leg bowing out.

One pant leg bows out due to high hip.

Repin pants to elastic until crease hangs straight.

1   Unpin the pants from the elastic at the side seam until the front crease hangs straight. Repin the pants to the elastic.

■ NOTE FROM NANCY

The higher hip has a greater curve, requiring more fabric to go around the shape. This causes the crease to hang outward unless you make fitting changes on the pattern. Try pinching a 1" tuck at your side seam and watch the pant crease (or the skirt side seam) bow to the side.

2   Take off the pants.

3   Mark the new waist stitching line on the pant front and back. Measure the changes and record them on the *Personal Fitting Chart for Pants*, page 123.

4   Make fitting changes on the pants.
- Lay the pants, right side up, on a flat surface.
- Match the front pattern piece to the cut edges of the side that has the high hip.
- Mark the new stitching line on the pattern, adding a ⅝" seam where needed. Indicate high hip side on the pattern.

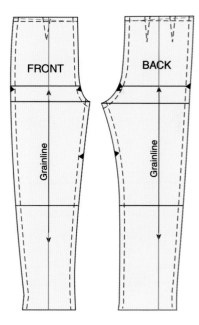

5   Attach the waistband, sewing a smaller seam allowance at the adjusted pant side.

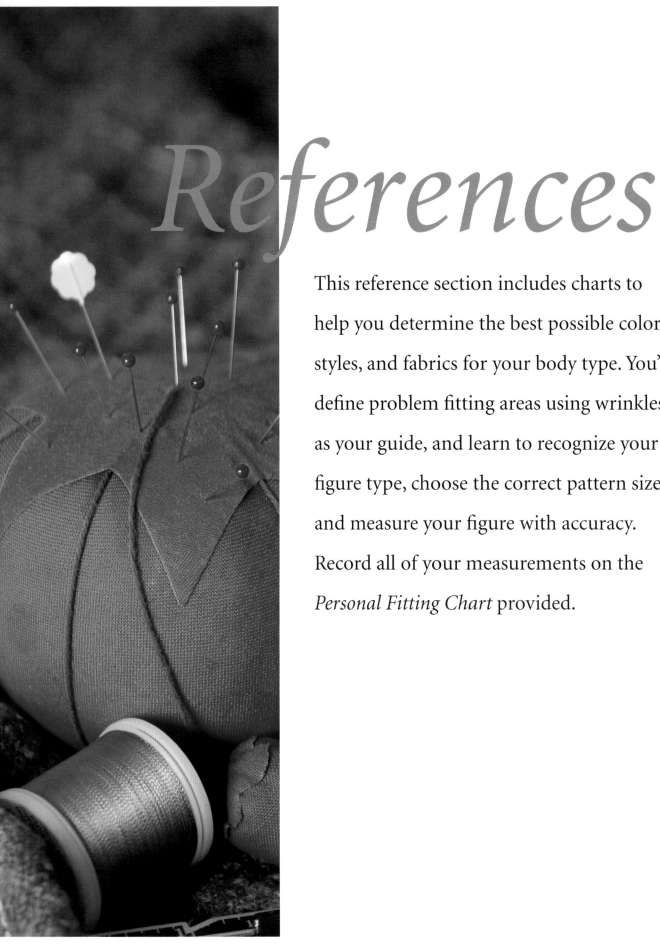

References

This reference section includes charts to help you determine the best possible colors, styles, and fabrics for your body type. You'll define problem fitting areas using wrinkles as your guide, and learn to recognize your figure type, choose the correct pattern size, and measure your figure with accuracy. Record all of your measurements on the *Personal Fitting Chart* provided.

BODY SILHOUETTE CHART

Description	Goal	Best Styles	Best Colors and Fabrics
Pear-shaped: Has greater width at hip than shoulder	Broaden shoulders and draw eyes away from hip	• Sleeves with pleats or gathers • Shoulder pads • Trims positioned to create vertical lines • Double-breasted jackets • Horizontal lines above waist • Vertical lines below waist for slimming effect—skirts with gores or pants with pleats • Jackets or tunics that end below fullest part of hip	• Textured fabrics and trims above waist to add volume and emphasis to upper body • Crisper fabrics, brighter colors above waist to draw eyes up • One-color outfits, adding emphasis above waist with buttons, trims, accessories (jewelry, scarves, etc.) • Two-tone outfits, with darker color for skirts or pants
Description	Goal	Best Styles	Best Colors and Fabrics
Full-busted: Has upside-down triangular shape, largest at bust	Balance top and bottom of figure to achieve illusion of proportioned silhouette	• Pattern lines to move eyes down, away from bust • Linear emphasis below waist— dropped waists, hip yokes with gathers below waist • Shoulder tucks or pleats to provide softness and add fullness, without emphasizing bust • Blouson tops to flatter figure stylishly and comfortably • Pants or skirts with fullness or weight below waist to create visual balance between top and bottom torso	• Solid-color tops with print or textured skirts • Smooth-textured fabrics without significant shine or luster above waist; textured fabrics below waist • Medium-weight fabrics above waist to conceal body curves • Allover prints with dark backgrounds

Styles for pear-shaped figures

Styles for full-busted figures

BODY SILHOUETTE CHART

Description	Goal	Best Styles	Best Colors and Fabrics
Full-figured: Has wide bust, waist, and hip in proportion to height	Create slimmer look using vertical lines to draw eyes up and down rather than across body	• Long tunic tops with front plackets • Blouson tops to create soft design lines • Loose fitting jackets or tops in lengths that end below the hip • U or V necks to visually draw attention up	• One-color outfits (not necessarily dark color) to coax eye up, make figure seem taller and more slender • Soft- to medium-weight fabrics to shape around curves without emphasizing body contours • Darker fabrics at heaviest or fullest part of body; lighter colors in slimmest area of body • Dull textures to minimize attention
Description	**Goal**	**Best Styles**	**Best Colors and Fabrics**
Long-waisted: Has added length in upper torso in proportion to bottom of figure	Visually shorten upper torso	• Yokes or wide collars to add width to upper body and visually shorten it • Pockets, epaulets, lapels to draw eye across body • Wide waistbands to shorten upper body	• Any fabric • Belt colors matched to garments to de-emphasize waistline • Belt colors matched to fabrics below waist to increase length of lower torso • Horizontal stripes, especially above waist, to shorten waist

Styles for full figures

Styles for long waisted figures

BODY SILHOUETTE CHART

Description	Goal	Best Styles	Best Colors and Fabrics
Short-waisted: Has short upper torso in relation to lower torso	Make upper torso appear longer in proportion to lower half of figure by visually adding length to upper body	• Dropped-waist styles to make body appear longer • Narrow collars, U or V necks to increase upper torso length • Princess styles to draw eye up and down • Vertical lines to visually add length	• Allover prints • Small-print fabrics above waist • Two-piece outfits in one color
Description	Goal	Best Styles	Best Colors and Fabrics
Petite: Has much shorter waist length than average, small bone structure, 5'3" or shorter height	Visually lengthen petite figure to make silhouette appear taller; achieve ⅓–⅔ division of figure (upper body to lower body) through use of colors and design features	• V necks, other vertical lines to draw eyes up and add length • Vertical lines plus horizontal lines to add height and fullness • Double-breasted garments to add fullness • Short jackets to keep figure in proportion • Tiered layers to add fullness • Short sleeves to create ⅓–⅔ proportions; long jackets with short skirts to create ⅔ to ⅓ reverse proportions	• Small- to medium-size prints with white or cream spaces between motifs to add light spaces and fullness • One-color outfits, with shoes and hosiery in neutral tone or matching skirt to add visual length • Combined design elements (vertical lines, color blocking) to draw eye up for height

Styles for short waisted figures

Styles for petite figures

BODY SILHOUETTE CHART

Description	Goal	Best Styles	Best Colors and Fabrics
Slim-Tall: Has small bone structure, height of 5'7" or taller, sometimes with longer waist length; may have athletic build, with broad shoulders and narrow bust, waist, and hip	Maximize the most versatile figure type by wearing a wide variety of patterns, styles	• Yokes, gathers, tucks, ruffles, pocket emphasis • Blouson tops to add curves; dropped waists to soften effect • Layering—combine jackets, vests, blouses, tunics • Dramatic dressing for both day and evening wear	• Textured fabric—bulky woolens, textured tweeds, prints, plaids, nubby fabrics • Accessories used as dramatic accents—large pins, chunky jewelry, big purses, scarves

RIGHT SIZE MEASUREMENT FITTING CHART

Measurement	12"	12½"	13"	13½"	14"	14½"	15"	15½"	16"	16½"	17"	17½"
Misses'/Miss Petite	6	8	10	12	14	16	18	20	22			
Juniors	5	7	9	11	13	15						
Women's/Women's Petite							38	40	42	44	46	48

WRINKLE CHART

Horizontal	Horizontal fold wrinkles = too much length	Horizontal pull wrinkles = not enough width
Vertical	Vertical fold wrinkles = too much width	Vertical pull wrinkles = not enough length
Bias	Bias fold wrinkles (combine vertical and horizontal) = too much length and width	Bias pull wrinkles (combine vertical and horizontal) = not enough length and width

If your finished garment has wrinkles, determine whether they are caused by too much fabric or too little fabric. Compare them to this chart and then turn to *Fine-Tuning the Fit*, beginning on page 102, for specific instructions on eliminating each type of wrinkle.

PERSONAL FITTING CHART

Name: Date:

Right Size Measurement: Pattern Type: Pattern Size:

	Bust	Waist	Hip	Back Waist Length	Back Width	Sleeve Length	Upper Arm	Special Meas.
Pattern Envelope Measurement								
- Your Measurement								
+ Additional Ease								
= Difference (+/-)								
Adjust? (Yes or No)								
Body Silhouette								
Best Styles								
Best Colors and Fabrics								

To use the *Personal Fitting Chart*, see pages 10–11 for how to take figure measurements and record them on the chart. Choose your correct size by using the *Right Size Measurement Fitting Chart*, page 9. Compare your figure measurements to the body measurements on the back of your pattern envelope to determine where you need to make fitting changes.

If you sew for more than one person, photocopy this chart for each person.

PERSONAL FITTING CHART FOR PANTS

Name: Date:

Pattern Type: Pattern Size:

	Length	Side Curve	Crotch	Waist	Hip	Thigh	Special Measurements
Pattern Envelope Measurement							
- Your Measurement (include ease)	no ease	no ease	no ease	+ 1" ease	+ 2" ease	+ 1" ease	
= Difference (+/-)							
Adjust? (Yes or No)							

To use the *Personal Fitting Chart for Pants*, see pages 75–77 for how to take figure measurements and record them on the chart. Choose your correct size by using the *Pant Pattern Size Chart*, below. Compare your figure measurements to the measurements on the back of the pattern envelope to determine where you need to make fitting changes.

In the Special Measurements column, record other information, such as the depth of wrinkles found in the fine-tuning process (see pages 106–115).

If you sew for more than one person, photocopy this chart for each person.

PANT PATTERN SIZE CHART

Hip Measurement	Misses'/Miss Petite	Juniors	Women's/Women's Petite
34"	6	5	
36"	8	7	
38"	10	9	
40"	12	11	
42"	14	13	
44"	16	15	38
46"	18		40
48"	20		42
50"+	22		44

Choose your correct pant size based on this chart. If your hips are larger than 50", use Misses' size 22 or Women's size 44.

Index

(NN)* denotes information contained in a Note from Nancy

Put Your Confidence in Nancy

Sew with Confidence
*A Beginner's Guide
to Basic Sewing*
by Nancy Zieman

Teaches basic sewing techniques and provides information on materials and tools needed to get started, sewing and serger machines, organizing the sewing area, patterns, fabrics and more.

Softcover • 8¼ x 10⅞ • 128 p
150 color photos, 100 illus.
Item# SWWC
0-87349-811-9 • **$21.99**

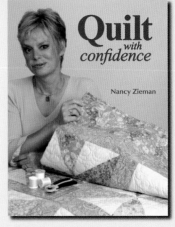

Quilt with Confidence
by Nancy Zieman

Leading sewing expert Nancy Zieman covers topics including tool selection, organizing the quilting area, rotary techniques, seaming and much more to give beginning quilters the confidence they need to keep quilting.

Softcover • 8¼ x 10⅞ • 144 p
50+ color photos;
500 color illus.
Item# Z1549
0-89689-593-9 • **$24.99**

Machine Embroidery with Confidence
A Beginner's Guide
by Nancy Zieman

Nancy Zieman explains the basics of machine embroidery including what tools to use, how to organize the embroidery area, types of machines, designs, templating/positioning, software, stabilizers, trouble shooting and finishing touches.

Softcover • 8¼ x 10⅞ • 144 p
100 color photos
Item# CFEM
0-87349-857-7 • **$21.99**

The Art of Landscape Quilting
by Nancy Zieman
and Natalie Sewell

This one-stop guide includes instructions for 16 upscale step-by-step projects and 20 partial projects; complete with tips, tricks and techniques for successfully designing and completing landscape quilts.

Softcover • 10 x 7 • 144 p
200 color photos
Item# LQCG • 0-89689-314-6 • **$24.99**

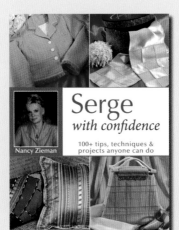

Serge with Confidence
by Nancy Zieman

Create stunning fashions, accessories and home décor items with more than 100 tips, techniques and projects featured in this must have resource. Learn skills for operating various sergers.

Softcover • 8¼ x 10⅞ • 128 p
315+ color photos and illus.
Item# CFSE • 0-87349-855-0
$22.99

Featured on
Sewing With Nancy®

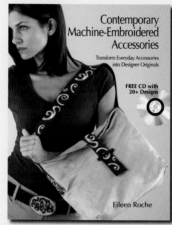

Contemporary Machine-Embroidered Accessories
Transform Everyday Accessories into Designer Originals
by Eileen Roche

Discover valuable secrets for using stabilizers and creating 18 exciting projects you can make and wear, including hats, scarves, belts, gloves and more, regardless of your size.

Softcover • 8¼ x 10⅞ • 128 p
250 color photos
Item# Z0762
0-89689-491-6 • $29.99

Embroidery Machine Essentials: Appliqué Techniques
Jeanine Twigg's Companion Project Series 4
by Mary Mulari

Appliqué expert Mary Mulari teaches innovative techniques for combining appliqué and machine embroidery. Features more than 20 fabulous projects on an included CD-ROM!

Softcover • 8¼ x 10⅞ • 48 p
100 color photos, plus illus.
Item# EMA
0-87349-847-X • $19.99

My Style, My Place
by Allyce King
and Nicole Thieret

Empower a young sewing sister to tap into her own individualistic and creative spirit and explore the possibilities of 25 quick do-it-yourself projects for the home and wardrobe.

Softcover • 8¼ x 10⅞ • 128 p
125 color photos
Item# Z0935
0-89689-538-6 • $24.99

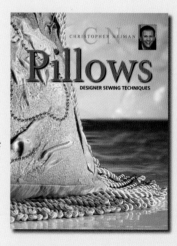

Christopher Nejman's Pillows
Designer Sewing Techniques
by Christopher Nejman

Follow charismatic instructor Christopher Nejman as he teaches you how to use your punch machine to create 15 stunning designer pillows, using various threads, fabrics and decorative stitches.

Softcover • 8¼ x 10⅞ • 128 p
225 color photos
Item# Z0304
0-89689-403-7 • $22.99

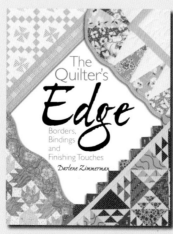

The Quilter's Edge
Borders, Bindings and Finishing Touches
by Darlene Zimmerman

Bring a fabulous finish to any quilt with more than 200 step-by-step instructional color photos covering techniques including scalloped edges, curved edges, notched edges and more.

Softcover • 8¼ x 10⅞ • 128 p
200+ color photos and illus.
Item# QLFT
0-87349-979-4 • $22.99

Sip 'n Sew
by Diane Dhein

Stitch delightful gifts for family and friends, while serving up delicious drinks, sure to tempt the taste buds! Features 24 projects for the home, along with 20 tasty drink recipes, all quick and easy to make.

Softcover • 8 x 8 • 160 p
75 color illus.
Item# Z0981
0-89689-552-1 • $19.99

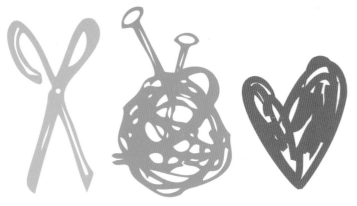

mycraftivity.com

CONNECT. CREATE. EXPLORE.

BEADING +
JEWELRY

SEWING
+ FASHION

KNITTING +
CROCHETING

QUILTING

INSPIRATION +
CREATIVITY

- Meet other crafters who share your interests
- Share your ideas, projects and perspective on crafting
- Get feedback on your projects from other crafters
- Learn about new books as soon as they are published
- Learn new techniques
- Free project ideas every week!

Visit mycraftivity.com today!

 krause publications
An imprint of F+W Publications, Inc.

 NORTH LIGHT BOOKS

 MEMORY MAKERS BOOKS

 D&C
David and Charles